SYMBOLISME FROM POE TO MALLARMÉ

Symbolisme from

POE

TO

MALLARMÉ

The Growth of a Myth

by

JOSEPH CHIARI
D.-ès-L.

FOREWORD BY
T. S. ELIOT

Second Edition

GORDIAN PRESS
NEW YORK
1970

First Edition Published 1956
Second Edition with Corrections
Published 1970

Library of Congress Catalog Card Number 76-114096
SBN 87752-020-8

Author's preface to the Second Edition

This book was written seventeen years ago, before the arrival of the first Americans on the Moon. The authors of *Eureka* and of *Un Coup de Dé,* were perhaps with them in spirit, for they were ever keen to project themselves out of the earth. First of all, I should like to express my gratitude to the *Gordian Press* for reprinting this book, and secondly, I should like to comment briefly on some of its aspects, which might require further elucidation.

Honour to whom it is due; I shall say a few words about the first sentence of the foreword, written by my dear friend, T. S. Eliot, which says: "it must be a book about a movement — the most important "movement" in the world of poetry since that of Wordsworth and Coleridge . . . . . ," and which could perhaps lead the reader to expectations which the author never intended to satisfy. This is primarily a book about the problem of literary influence and about the question as to whether Mallarmé's poetry could be said to have been influenced by the poetry and the literary writings of Edgar A. Poe; therefore, though the symbolist movement, its aesthetics and its members, will be seriously discussed, it is not an exhaustive study of Symbolism. Then, still dealing with the same foreword, I should like to comment upon the sentence which says: "Without this aesthetic I do not think that the work of some modern writers would be quite what it is (I am thinking of Rilke, for example, and of some of my own later work) . . . . ." This is a statement which falls within the pattern of Eliot's well known view, which is that every important work of art necessarily modifies the whole conspectus of art which preceded it. This simply means that the existence of any given work of art necessarily plays a part in the creativity of any artist who works in the medium to which this work of art belongs. Baudelaire no more wanted to be Victor Hugo than T. S. Eliot wanted to be Dante, whom he greatly admired. He used with great difficulties (according to himself) the terza rima, in a passage of *Little Gidding,* but of course, this stanzaic form is not the property of Dante. Many poets, including Shelley, in *"The Triumph of Life,"* and other modern poets have used it, in order to express their own sensibility. *Little Gidding* is, through and through, typical of Eliot's sensibility, and nobody else could have produced this transparent to and fro between fire and ice, which is also his masterpiece.

This type of relationship between an author and the works which preceded him, is not, therefore a question of influence or imitation, but a question of taking into account the existence of an already un-covered truth. The experience of an old man *"Among Schoolchildren"* has been given organic and final form by W. B. Yeats and any modern poet setting about to express, in his own terms, a similar experience will have to be most careful to avoid summoning any aspect of Yeat's poem, a comparison with which would not be to his advantage, and which could, in fact, make his own stillborn. Goethe and Schiller had great mutual admiration, were great friends, and they discussed at length their work in their correspondence, yet, however much they had in common each remained entirely faithful to his own essence and the tragic genius of the one was never interchangeable with the epic genius of the other. *Faust, Iphygenie, Herman and Dorothea* on one side, *Maria Stuart, Wallenstein* and the *Maid of Orleans* on the other remain each faithful to the dominant aspect of the genius of their author, unaffected by his admiration for his friend.

The question of influence in art is a very difficult one. A large part of the work of art faculties would cease to exist if the search for influences, as it is practised now, were shown to be, on the whole, unreal and worthless in works of genius. A commercially minded, a notoriety or fame-seeking artist, endowed with the talent to seize upon the mood and fashion of the moment and with the art to express them, will make use of forms, structures, characters, themes and situations which he knows to be conducive to the aims he has in mind. This type of artist, more common and widespread than the true discoverer of truth, will make use of his gifts to assimilate and to lift up from all sources, the ingredients which will enable him to create the object which will satisfy a demand or meet with a coveted reward. He will therefore be guided by a pre-existing concept and not by the urge or the desire to discover an as yet uncovered truth.

This broad division of artists into two main categories could, and ought to be clarified by a long exposition as to what is meant by conceptualism and also on the degree of consciousness and, therefore, of conceptualism which obtains in the case of the works of genius. This would be beyond the scope of a preface,

vii

which can only cover one or two aspects of these problems. Conceptualism in art is basically the antithesis of imagination. The concept is the ideal schema, pattern or essential structure of the object which the maker endeavors to produce, in order to meet a given requirement, or to reach a given aim. The task it presides over, is fundamentally, even if it is to produce pleasure or entertainment, a utilitarian one, and fantasy, and not imagination is the faculty which supplies the adornments, the frills and the assets which enhance the commercial value and attraction of the object produced. In the work of genius, it is not the concept always axled upon a very conscious ego, which is the guiding light of artistic creation, but the imagination, intent upon discovering individuated and universal essence. If the concept implies predetermination and strict guiding lines, the imagination does not imply, by contrast, random forces and random directions. The imagination is the intuitive faculty which enables genius to apprehend through the fusion of his own essence with the important aspects of the age in which he lives, the real truth or essence of that age. The themes which the artist of genius seeks to exteriorise or to give existence in symbolic entities, are those which contain the dominant forms of his self and are at the same time, according to the range of his genius part of the dominant forms of his age. These forms can be expressed by great artists as well as by great philosophers. That is why French, English and German Romantics echo, in varying degrees, Rousseau, Hegel, Schelling and Schopenhauer, and that is why, with the time gap which separates French sensibility from German and British sensibility, Mallarmé and Valéry truly echo Hegel only during the latter part of the nineteenth century, while Goethe and Schiller his contemporaries, at times echo him, and at times anticipate him.

Wordsworth did not set about to write the *Lyrical Ballads* in order to meet a given demand or to try to achieve a given aim. He wrote them because endowed with imagination as he was, he could sense that the profound truth of his time was represented not by poetry and art as means to adorn, to distract or to comfort the life of the well satisfied middle-class, but by art as the expression of vital human forces, simmering under the surface and demanding expression in order to alter the course of the social evolution. Language, with him and with the poets of his own calibre of imagination, ceases being a disguise, or a lulling device, to become what it always is with the imagination, a means of discovering and forging truths, which once quarried out of the depth of humankind are destined to illumine its progress, or rather, the movement of transformation of matter into spirit.

Both conceptual and imaginative art, that is to say true art, are related in different ways to society and to the time when they come to life. The former only corresponds to the surface which is froth, foam, eddies and conflicting ripples which do not prevent the flow of life from moving in its given direction and from being continually stimulated on its course, by the truth of art which makes it more and more conscious of its course. 'Genie echo de soi sans commencement ni chute, simultané en le delice de son intuition superieure', said Mallarmé. As a genius Mallarmé's essence is to be himself, that is to say to reveal through existence, the imaginative relationship between his essential themes and the essential themes of the age in which he lived. These revelations are fragments of eternal truth, and, irrespective of the fact that when they appeared, they were only hailed and praised by the few, they have greater historical and ontological significance for the life and development of mankind than the immensely successful plays of Scribe the novels of Eugene Sue, or the academic painting of the time. To believe that symbolism and together with it, that Baudelaire's, Mallarmé's and Valéry's ideas and themes could be diochronically derived from Poe or any other father or fount and not synchronous to the age in which these writers lived, is of the same order as believing that the whole of mankind was derived from one single Adam supposedly born six thousand years ago.

The ideas which constitute the main tenets of symbolism were part of the climate of the age and therefore directly intuited by the various artists involved, and not derived through filiations from one eponymous hero who could be said to be responsible for them. The attitude of these artists mirrors the society in which they are living and expresses the basic essences of this society. The great French Revolution, this unique historical explosion of Romanticism and Rationalism, had not been paralleled by anything similar in the arts. Napoleon the archetypal hero of the Revolution, could say at the age of twenty-nine "I need solitude and isolation grandeur wearies me; the fount of feeling is dried up; glory itself is insipid. At twenty-nine years of age I have exhausted everything. It only remains for me to become a thorough egoist". French art of the time, was neither Goethean nor Byronic; it was turned towards Greece, the land of freedom and democracy, the land of heroes. Of course,

Byron admired Greece and Goethe, Schiller and Hölderlin sought to renew in Germany, just as it was
done in France, the neo-classical spirit. But, Goethe,
Schiller and Hölderlin were great poets who blended
both neo-classicism and Romanticism, while in France,
during the same period poetry was at a very low ebb
and looked even more so, by comparison with the
great blossoming which took place in Great Britain.
Imagination in France, seemed to be devoted to war-
like activities and was practically dead in poetry. It
had been so, in fact, right through the eighteenth century, during which reason and sentiments had been
uppermost in French art, while imagination had remained what Pascal had described as: "la folle du
logis". The truth is that French society, that is to say
the society which both supplied artists and was interested in the arts, was essentially rationalistic, sentimental, and distrustful of strong individualism, fierce
passions, or of artistic creations which were not strictly
rational and reassuring. In Great Britain, imagination,
right from the Renaissance, had neither lost its hold on
people, nor its pre-eminence in the arts, and while
France had her political revolution, Great Britain had
her artistic revolution aimed at rejuvenating language
and the themes of poetry, and at shaking the social
conscience in the face of man's inhumanity to man.
The realistic poetry of Burns, Wordsworth and Coleridge and the combination of realism and vision of
Blake, all stress the primacy of the imagination. In
France, one had to wait for Baudelaire's time to hear
the same assertion. French Romanticism, above all,
explored new themes according to old rules of rhetoric
and conceptualism. Sentiments which had been one of
the main preoccupations of eighteenth century art had

become even more so with Romanticism, and "le moi", which Pascal and the Classicists had banned from art and from the life of the "honnete homme", as "haissable", became the very foundation of Romantic art. "Le Moi", of course is the heart, and the artist's main aim is to let his heart speak, that is to say to spill out his feelings. "Ah frappe-toi le Coeur, c'est lá qu'est le genie", said Musset whose allegory of the Pelican feeding his young ones with its own substance, is the best representation and description of the Romantic poet, from Chateaubriand to Lamartine and Hugo. To give one's heart to the crowd, to suffer and to wear one's own sorrows round one's neck for everyone to see, these are the themes of poetry, illustrated once more by Musset, who said: "Rien ne nous rend si grand qu'une grande douleur".

Vigny alone of the great Romantics protested against what he considered to be a lack of nerve and dignity, and he rejoins Le Conte de Lisle in his refusal to hand over his heart to the carniverous mob. The notion that sadness, sorrows and suffering can be the best sources of song, is nowhere absent from English poetry from Keats and Shelley to Yeats, but English or Irish never departed from moderation and realism. They shunned rhetoric and excessive exuberance, and they continuously retained a sense of mystery, of darkness and shades and subtle impression which call forth the creativeness of the reader or hearer. Though one must not completely ignore the fact that the "I", "le moi" was anything but absent from the poetry of Keats and Shelley and that Keats had described Wordsworth as "The egotistical sublime". In France, we have to wait for symbolism to see these new attitudes towards art prevail. The eloquence of Lamartine and Musset is different from that of Corneille; it extols feelings instead of reason, honour, and control but it lasted until Verlaine decided to wring its neck, and Baudelaire chose to give the every day, banal life of Paris, the imprint of a chastened subtle, imageladen style, which transformed French poetry.

By the latter half of the nineteenth century, once the wave of the great novelists and Romantic poets and painters had settled down, the arts in France, are, above all, entertainment, or decoration for the bourgeois who ignores them, unless they conform to its taste, which is academism in painting, and superficial writing in the novel and in poetry. "The novel" has become according to Hegel "the modern bourgeois epic . . . . . ", and by and large, it has taken the place of poetry which is only appreciated by the few and by the initiated. The novel is now naturalistic, with Zola and the Goncourts as its master. So is the theatre, so is a great deal of painting, including Impressionism. Poetry echoes Balzac's and Flaubert's realism with Baudelaire, and on the other hand, moves on to pure idealism with Mallarmé who said: "To paint, not the thing itself, but the effect it produces"; a definition which could be applied to 'cubism'. Poe, the "poete maudit", the apostle of suggestiveness and mystery, described by Emerson as "the jingle man", and by Whitman as "perpetuate chimes of music bells, ringing from lower b flat up to g, the author of tales of imagination and mystery which could titillate the jaded palate of the bourgeois, only had in common with Mallarmé, the fully confessed admiration which the latter had for him. Mallarmé himself never said that Poe influenced him; he on the contrary said "the poet feeds upon his own secret and well-established

individuality, rather than on external circumstances".[1]
Mallarmé was not interested in dandyism, attitudiniz-
ing drinks, or drugs, in order to shock or to forget the
crowd. He was on a higher metaphysical plane; he was
master of his destiny, his own father, creator of his
transcendental self, through poetry, and only the initiated, those equipped with special means could watch
his flights upward, from darkness to light, from nothingness to self created transcendence. If there is one
thinker who may have strengthened and comforted
him in his attitude towards artistic creation, it is Hegel
with whose work Mallarmé was acquainted, but with
whom he had above all great affinities and whom he
described as "le Titan de l'esprit humain, Hegel".[2] He
shares with Hegel the very basis of his aesthetics which
are the creativity of nothingness, the search for the
absolute, which Mallarmé calls "l'idée" and the notion
of poetry as means of abstracting and turning the particular and the finite, into the Universal, an operation
which Hegel sums up in the following terms: "Besides,
poetry, by the very fact that its mode of expression is
language, always represents in a general way. The
essence of the word is to abstract and to sum up. In
general, poetry, the task of poetry is to free the essential and significant element which contains energy, and
this element is precisely the ideal."[3] The world, matter,
and things are, with Mallarmé, replaced by, or transmuted into the idea; they are aspired up by a kind of
nothingness which dissolves materially and replaces it
by the poet's transcendental "I", intent upon the universal, the absolute. All this takes place musically, for
every soul is a melody which has to reconnect with the

1. Mallarmé, oeuvre comp. p. 876.
2. Op cit. p. 386.
3. Hegel Esthetique, Ed. Bernard I. p. 68.

universal, and music is a pentecostal fire which lifts it towards the light, one of the obsessions of Mallarmé. Light or consciousness, or, as Hegel put it "Light is parallel with the consciousness of self and is, in some ways, its faithful image . . . . . If the "I" could maintain itself in a state of pure equilibrium within itself, a state which the Hindus endeavor to reach, it would fade away, it would no longer be the "I" but the light, the abstract and transparent being".[4] From nothingness to the transcendental act which is both the poet and the poem, from silence to silence, the poet annihilates himself and matter into a tongue of flames and the duration of the poem is all. Silence explodes into the multicoloured inter connected fragments which are the words, illuminating the sky and fading away into darkness. And over and over again; "Victorieusement fui le suicide beau", the process begins again, an Appolo-like journey, a repeated suicide, a God-like act in a God deserted age, which is the age of Mallarmé.

---

4. Hegel Philosophy of Nature I, p. 34

Joseph Chiari

Foreword

By T. S. ELIOT

THIS is a book about the poet Mallarmé, but the author has done well to entitle it ". . . from Poe to Mallarmé": for a book about Mallarmé must also be a book about Poe and about Baudelaire, and must not ignore Mallarmé's most illustrious disciple, Paul Valéry. It must be a book about a movement—the most important "movement" in the world of poetry since that of Wordsworth and Coleridge—and about the æsthetics of that movement.

I must surround the term "movement" with safeguards of several kinds. To say that this is the most important poetic movement since Wordsworth and Coleridge is not to exaggerate the individual importance of the poets involved in it, or to place them higher than other poets, in France, England, and other countries, who are outside of it. Nor can the term here have any of its popular associations. We usually think of a literary movement as a group of young enthusiastic writers who issue a manifesto; who have or who pretend to have certain principles in common; whose work is likely to show a family resemblance; and who are banded together in championship of a common cause, or for sociability and mutual comfort, or at worst for purposes of collective self-advertisement. We think of a "movement" as a phenomenon of youth, and we expect that the sturdier members will in time leave the group as they develop their individual styles, and that the weaker members will disappear into oblivion. By "movement", here, I mean a continuity of admiration: Baudelaire admired Poe, Mallarmé admired Poe and Baudelaire, Valéry admired Poe and Baudelaire and Mallarmé—and a continuity of development of poetic theory. Valéry was the disciple of Mallarmé: but there was no personal association among the rest. Mallarmé, I have been told, came to Paris because Baudelaire was there: he once saw Baudelaire at a bookstall on a quay, but had not the courage to address him. And of course Baudelaire never met Poe. And, as Mr. Chiari points out, although each of these French poets in turn found Poe intensely stimulating, there is no evidence of imitation or even of borrowing from Poe in their work.

How far Baudelaire would have been Baudelaire, or Mallarmé Mallarmé, without the stimulus provided by Poe, is a question to which the answer can never be more than conjecture; but Mr. Chiari is right to raise the question, and leave it in our minds. To Anglo-Saxon readers it must seem that this paradoxical "movement", in which the poets from generation to generation were not greatly influenced by each other's poetry, but deeply influenced by each other's attitude towards poetry, was largely propelled by an initial misunderstanding. It is difficult for us to see how three French poets, all men of exceptional intellectual gifts, could have taken Poe so seriously as a philosopher—for it is Poe's theories about poetry, rather than his poems, that meant most to them. How good a poet was Poe? There is no poet whose status is more disputed. And as a philosopher? It is difficult for an English or American reader to regard as anything but extravagant the praise which Valéry lavishes upon *Eureka*. We suspect, indeed, that if the French poets had known the English language better they could not have rated Poe so high as a stylist; and that if they had known English literature better they might have based their aesthetics not on that of Poe but on that of Coleridge.

No matter: if the influence of Poe upon Baudelaire, Mallarmé and Valéry was based upon misunderstanding, it was a fecund and significant misunderstanding; for the aesthetic which they erected upon this dubious foundation remains valid for their own work. The time had come for a new attitude towards poetry, on the part of poets first, to be accepted by readers afterwards. It does not matter whether Poe's account of the composition of *The Raven* was a conscious hoax, or whether Poe was hoaxing himself; what it suggested to the French poets was an aesthetic which might have come into existence in some other way, if Poe had never written or if Baudelaire had never read Poe.

Any good poet, of course, can be enjoyed without our having previously informed ourselves about his relation to other poets, and without our knowing anything about his theory of poetry—if he has one. Indeed, if this were not so, we might doubt whether what he had written was poetry at all. What we get from a study of these French poets in relation to Poe, is an understanding of their aesthetic which enlarges our understanding of their poetry. And by "aesthetic" here I do not mean merely an abstract theory of what poetry should be; I mean an attitude to poetry, by poets of great critical capacity, which has affected indirectly a good deal of poetry written since and which has also affected the attitude of readers towards their poetry. What the reader of poetry has come to expect of modern poetry, and the way in which he is prepared to enjoy it, are partly due to the attitude of these French poets to their own work. Without this aesthetic I do not think that the work of some other modern writers would be quite what it is (I am thinking of Rilke, for example, and of some of my own later work) or that, if it was the same, it would find a public prepared for it.

This, of course, is not the whole story. Baudelaire would have been a great poet in any case, a greater than Poe; and much more became possible because of Baudelaire—I am thinking of Laforgue, Corbière and Rimbaud—than is found in the poetic current examined in this book. But this poetic current represents a peculiar development of self-consciousness in the poetry of the last hundred years. Mr. Chiari, who is at home in both languages and with both literatures, English and French, and who has examined the voluminous critical literature of his subject in French, has performed a useful service in giving us the first book in English on Mallarmé and his art of poetry.

T. S. ELIOT

Contents

Une brève réflexion fait connaître qu'il n'y a pas d'autre parti que l'on puisse prendre. Il faut se mettre sciemment à la place de l'être qui nous occupe. . . . C'est notre propre fonctionnement qui, *seul*, peut nous apprendre quelque chose sur toute chose. . . . C'est avec notre propre substance que nous imaginons et que nous formons une pierre, une plante, un mouvement, un *objet*: une image quelconque n'est peut-être qu'un commencement de nous-mêmes. . . .

PAUL VALÉRY, *Introduction à la méthode de Léonard de Vinci*—
Note et Digression

Soit que nous nous élevions jusqu'aux cieux, soit que nous descendions jusque dans les abîmes, nous ne sortons jamais de nous-mêmes, et ce n'est que notre propre pensée que nous apercevons: or, c'est là le résultat du premier dialogue de Berkeley, et le fondement de tout son systeme.

DIDEROT, *Lettre sur les aveugles*

Tel qu'en Lui-même enfin l'éternité le change,
Le Poète suscite avec un glaive nu
Son siècle épouvanté de n'avoir pas connu
Que la mort triomphait dans cette voix étrange!

Eux, comme un vil sursaut d'hydre oyant jadis l'ange
Donner un sens plus pur aux mots de la tribu
Proclamèrent très haut le sortilège bu
Dans le flot sans honneur de quelque noir mélange.

Du sol et de la nue hostiles, ô grief!
Si notre idée avec ne sculpte un bas-relief
Dont la tombe de Poe éblouissante s'orne.

Calme bloc ici-bas chu d'un désastre obscur
Que ce granit du moins montre à jamais sa borne
Aux noirs vols du Blasphème épars dans le futur.

MALLARMÉ, *Le Tombeau d'Edgar Poe*

CHAPTER I

Introduction

"IN his theory and practice Mallarmé was the conclusion and crown of the Symbolist Movement."[1] "But a more important prophet of Symbolism was Edgar Allan Poe . . . and one of the events of prime importance in the early history of the Symbolist Movement was the discovery of Poe by Baudelaire. . . . In 1852, Baudelaire published a volume of translations of Poe's tales; and from then on the influence of Poe played an important part in French literature. Poe's critical writings provided the first scriptures of the Symbolist Movement, for he had formulated what amounted to a new literary programme which corrected the Romantic looseness and lopped away the Romantic extravagance, at the same time that it aimed, not at Naturalistic, but at ultra-Romantic effects."[2] These are two widely accepted opinions, and the aim of this study will be to investigate the historical support which one can discover for or against them. This will therefore be a study of the problem of literary influence with regard to literary movements and in particular with regard to the influence of one writer—Poe— upon one of his followers—Mallarmé. In order to see Mallarmé's relationship to symbolism and Poe's relationship to symbolism and to Mallarmé, one needs first to know, not symbolism in all its manifestations, but its roots—which, if one wishes to follow them up, go as far back as history—and its main tenets, the exposition of which should underlie the similarities and the differences between Poe's and Mallarmé's

[1] C. M. Bowra, *The Heritage of Symbolism* (Macmillan, London), p. 1.
[2] Edmund Wilson, *Axël's Castle* (Charles Scribner's Sons, New York, 1948), p. 12.

I

poetry and æsthetics. After that, as my primary concern is not Mallarmé's poetry in isolation but Mallarmé's relation to Poe and to symbolism, I shall proceed with the evidence from critics and from Mallarmé himself; then I shall examine Poe's æsthetics in order to detect its main traits and to see how far it resembles, or has influenced, Mallarmé's; next I shall examine Mallarmé's poetry not as a creative process, but purely from the point of view of evidence of Poe's influence on that poetry, and finally suggest a conclusion.

The case of Edgar Allan Poe is one of the most puzzling in literature.   On one hand we have a poet who, in the English-speaking world, is considered as a minor one with a very negligible influence. "Emerson and Henry James thought him small change and according to F. O. Matthiessen, no other American critic of standing has contradicted those two mighty arbiters of literary value."[1] Yet one may remember that Tennyson looked upon him as "the most original American genius",[2] that W. B. Yeats thought he was "a great lyric poet",[3] and that T. S. Eliot thinks that Poe was "a man of very exceptional mind and sensibility"[4] and that he was unquestionably a poet. These are testimonies which nobody can brush aside, for they have behind them the authority of three of the most important poets of the last hundred years. Above all, there is the fact that in Europe, and particularly in France, from the days of Baudelaire to ours, Poe has been looked upon as a major poet and acknowledged as one of the greatest literary influences of our time. The prediction of the Goncourt brothers, who, seven years after his death, wrote in their *Journal*: "Here is the literature of the twentieth century!" has, in appearance at least, been fulfilled. Three major French

---

[1] Montgomery Belgion, 'The Mystery of Poe', *Essays in Criticism* (Basil Blackwell), vol. I, no. 1, January 1951, p. 51.
[2] Ibid., p. 66.   [3] Ibid., p. 66.
[4] *From Poe to Valéry* (Harcourt, Brace and Company, New York, 1948), p. 19.

poets—Baudelaire, Mallarmé and Valéry—representing three successive generations of French poetry, have acknowledged the greatness of Poe and submitted in turn, and directly, to the influence of his poetry and of his critical writings. Nobody, nowadays, questions the eminence of Baudelaire, Mallarmé or Valéry as poets, each one of them undeniably a much greater poet than Poe; and each one of them having acknowledged him as a master and 'a great poet'. Anglo-Saxon critics suggest that, through their incomplete grasp of the English language, the French poets in question saw in Poe something which was not there and which was their own projection. This latter hypothesis is always partially true; the former could also be true in the case under examination; yet, on the other hand, "we should be prepared to entertain the possibility that these Frenchmen have seen something in Poe that English-speaking readers have missed".[1] Therefore we should approach the problem of Poe's influence on a poet like Mallarmé with an open mind.

The problem of influence in poetry is a very vexed one; "the greatest debts are not always the most evident".[2] Or, as Dr. Leavis says: "What one great original artist learns from another whose genius and problems are necessarily very different is the hardest kind of influence to define."[3] There are apparent influences which a poet can trace:

> I can name positively certain poets whose work has influenced me, I can name others whose work, I am sure, has not; there may be still others of whose influence I am unaware, but whose influence I might be brought to acknowledge: but about Poe I shall never be sure.[4]

> Of some poets I can say I learned a great deal from them at a particular stage. Of Jules Laforgue, for instance, I can

---

[1] T. S. Eliot, op cit., p. 7.
Vide, in our time, the admiration which the French have for Charles Morgan and Laurence Durrell, whose reputations in England, are in a much lower key.
[2] T. S. Eliot: 'Talk on Dante', *The Adelphi*, first quarter, 1951, p. 106.
[3] *The Great Tradition* (Chatto and Windus, London, 1948), p. 9.
[4] T. S. Eliot: *From Poe to Valéry*, p. 6.

say that he was the first to teach me how to speak, to teach me the poetic possibilities of my own idiom of speech. Such early influences, the influences which, so to speak, first introduce one to oneself, are, I think, due to an impression which is, in one aspect, the recognition of a temperament akin to one's own, and in another aspect the discovery of a form of expression which gives a clue to the discovery of one's own form. These are not two things, but two aspects of the same thing. But the poet who can do this for a young writer is unlikely to be one of the great masters. The latter are too exalted and too remote. They are like distant ancestors who have been almost deified; whereas the smaller poet, who has directed one's first steps, is more like an admired elder brother.[1]

This is a passage which, amongst other things, gives an interesting hint as to why, in France for instance, the poets who are supposed to have had the greatest influence are not the truly great ones—like Shakespeare, Milton or Wordsworth—but rather the secondary ones like Poe, Byron or Ossian. The great ones are too awe-inspiring; one gazes at them in admiration, but one does not dare to imitate them, one knows that the attempt would be a failure; nevertheless, their influence, in an indirect way, is probably greater than the conscious influence of the small ones, and certainly much greater than one realises. For, as Valéry says:

Qu'il s'agisse de la science ou des arts, on observe, si l'on s'inquiète de la génération des résultats, que toujours *ce qui se fait* répète *ce qui fut fait*, ou le réfute; le répète en d'autres *tons*, l'épure, l'amplifie, le simplifie, le charge ou le surcharge,—ou bien le rétorque, l'extermine, le renverse, le nie, mais donc le suppose, et l'a invisiblement utilisé. Le contraire naît du contraire.[2]

[1] T. S. Eliot: 'Talk on Dante', pp. 106–7.
[2] 'Lettre sur Mallarmé', reproduced in J. Royère, *Mallarmé* (Albert Messein, Paris, 1931), p. 9.

4

These views of Valéry are obviously true for science as well as for the arts like music, painting, sculpture, and, of course, in a restricted way, because of the barrier of language, in the field of poetry. The developments which take place in music or in painting and science are not limited to any country in particular; they transcend national frontiers because they are based on symbols and signs which every civilised human being can, in varying degree, understand. It is not the same with poetry, even in spite of the help of translations. Finally, one cannot dissociate poetry from the language in which it originated; so that the achievements, for instance, of Shakespeare, of Milton, or of any other great English poet, require for their appreciation, not only the prerequisite of imagination, but also a very profound knowledge of the English language, of its traditions and of English civilisation.

Every poet resembles other poets and yet is different from them. He resembles them in his function; he is different in the way he carries it out. He cannot ignore what preceded him, yet he cannot repeat it; he must go further, detach himself from what is before him, yet always be aware of the fact that what is before him has undeniably modified the sensibility of the society which gave it birth and the general landscape of history. Therefore he must fit within that landscape. He must not, and, in fact, cannot be alien to it, for he uses a medium—language—which is the memory of a people and also part of the memory of mankind, and yet he must be in some ways something of his own, something which indicates a growth. But why try to outline in a vague and incomplete way what has already been so clearly stated by an outstanding poet and critic? It seems to me that I cannot do better than quote what T. S. Eliot says on this subject in his Introduction to the *Selected Poems* of Ezra Pound:

Poets may be divided into those who develop technique, those who imitate technique, and those who invent technique. When I say 'invent', I should use inverted commas, for invention would be irreproachable if it were possible. 'Invention' is wrong only because it is impossible. ... The poem which is absolutely original is absolutely bad; it is, in the bad sense, 'subjective' with no relation to the world to which it appeals. Originality, in other words, is by no means a simple idea in the criticism of poetry. True originality is merely development; and if it is right development it may appear in the end so *inevitable* that we almost come to the point of view of denying all 'original' virtue to the poet.[1]

This, to my mind, makes it clear that there is no true originality in life or its emanation—the arts; at the same time, it does not lay any stress whatsoever on influence or imitation. In fact, in a theory of development and conscious growth like the one propounded by T. S. Eliot, and to which I subscribe, the problem of influence is integrated into the vaster process of unavoidable growth, a process which, in so far as what preceded unavoidably determines what followed, gives full scope to direct and above all to indirect influence. Knowledge cannot but modify one's sensibility and personality; but the crux is that knowledge is an essentially subjective experience, that we only know what we live through—what we explore imaginatively with our whole being thoroughly involved in the process. Although a certain affective knot such as, for instance, the one which holds together Hamlet's situation, has been crystallised into words, and therefore given concreteness, we cannot hope to get even a very moderate grasp of its vast implications, unless we have the imagination and the affective range to live subjectively, as much as possible, the experience contained in the play.

Together with the idea of organic growth which characterises life and all that pertains to it, another point to be borne

[1] *Selected Poems* of Ezra Pound (Faber and Faber, 1928), pp. x–xi.

in mind is the one brought out by a quotation from Coleridge's
preface to his poem, *Christabel*: "For there is amongst us a set
of critics, who seem to hold, that every possible thought and
image is traditional; who have no notion that there are such
things as fountains in the world, small as well as great; and
who would therefore charitably derive every rill they behold
flowing, from a perforation made in some other man's tank."[1]
Coleridge's thought exhibits throughout a fundamental belief
in transcendence which makes of Truth an absolute which
can have many forms in the temporal: "in geometry, it is the
universal truth itself, which is uppermost in the consciousness,
in poetry the individual form in which the truth is clothed".[2]

Heidegger, in the famous essay 'Hölderlin and the Essence
of Poetry', quotes Hölderlin as saying: "But that which
remains is established by the poets", and goes on to explain
that poetry is the act of establishing, by the word and in the
word, the permanent. Heidegger says that: "Being must be
opened out, so that the existent may appear. . . . The poet
names the gods and names all things in that which they are."[3]
This meets the idea of the permanent, the eternal *fountains* of
Coleridge and Wordsworth, or the *mothers* of Goethe, and
curtails considerably the problem of influence in true poetry.
Another point to be borne in mind, in an attempt to assess
influence, is that translations and quotations are not by any
means synonymous with influence. To take one single instance,
Chaucer had read Dante and we can easily find in his work
traces of direct translation from the *Divina Commedia*, yet there
is surely nothing more different from that poem than the
Canterbury Tales.

Influence is, of course, possible, and exists at the level of
technique; a poet can learn from another how to use certain
effects and how to perfect a certain form; in short, he can learn

---

[1] *Coleridge* (The Nonesuch Press, 1950), p. 58.
[2] *Biographia Literaria*, ed. J. Shawcross (1817), vol. ii, p. 159.
[3] *Existence and Being* (The Vision Press, 1949), p. 304.

2

his craft as every artist has to do; he can also be forewarned by the example of predecessors and therefore avoid, thanks to them, certain pitfalls. All technical aspects of the work of art can be assessed quite easily, yet the assessment does not contribute much towards solving the mystery of artistic creation. Rimbaud and Keats, for instance, seem to have been born with enough craft to enable them to say practically from the start what they had to say; all knowledge possible about 'form' cannot tell us why a twelve-syllable line by Racine is alive and one of the same length by Voltaire is generally dead. One can talk of influence at the superficial level of form, meaning the shape or phenomenal aspect of experience; yet such a separation is only possible in a conceptual type of poetry which has nothing much to do with true poetry in which the form is all. Besides, when one talks of 'influences', even at the superficial level of one poet being attracted by another, one forgets the fundamental fact that there must be some ineluctable compulsion which bends the gazer towards the gazed-at and links them both in a way which is part of the order of nature, whose effects we can describe but whose inner working eludes us. The themes which preoccupy a creative artist are his own; it does not mean that they are nobody else's in his time or in any other historical time, but it means that they are an inherent part of what forms his self. The fact that somebody has already dealt with them can only have an influence on him in so far as it warns him not to try to repeat what has already been done. Form being the expression, the only imitation or influence possible is at what Hopkins described as the Parnassian level, but not at the level of true inspiration or genius, which, as Coleridge said, "cannot be lawless . . . and is the power of acting creatively under laws of its own origination".

A very great illusion would be to believe that Professor Livingston Lowes' remarkable book *The Road to Xanadu* had solved the problem. This book is an excellent piece of detective work, illuminating about Coleridge's readings and interests, but it does not tell us anything about what Professor Lowes himself calls once more the 'shaping spirit'; it is as if we were shown Leonardo da Vinci's studio, with all the paints, brushes and canvases, and books which he had read—even more, with his whole life explained to us; yet from all that we should not be able to say how this and many years' work and reflections became *Mona Lisa* or *The Last Supper*. *The Road to Xanadu* has unfortunately encouraged a trend which is in some ways a reinstatement of Taine's doctrine, and which consists in trying to explain a work of art by the various readings, interests, heredity and nationality of the author, while a work of art is above all, as the great German idealists have suggested, an act of 'disinterestedness', an intuitive grasp of the unchanging essence in the light of the spirit which is genius. It can be apprehended as object by a thinking and feeling subject, it can be subjectively described and given a place in universals, but it cannot be explained any more than the very essence of life, to which it belongs, can be explained. The intellect can verify, infer or deduce from the moment of vision, source of knowledge, or lead up to it through patient research, but it cannot tell how to make it. Artistic masterpieces as well as great scientific discoveries rest on such unexplainable moments. Archimedes, Newton, Einstein and even Descartes, the author of the *Discours de la Méthode*, reached the bedrock of their various systems in moments of vision or pure intuition, and they all did so, not as pragmatists whose beliefs are confined to sense data and analytical truth, but as men possessed by metaphysical beliefs and aware that sequential reason cannot produce the moment of vision born from the intense and disinterested contemplation of objects and complexes of forces seeking expression in objectified individuations bearing the imprint of universality.

CHAPTER II

Symbolisme

" If God exists," says Kirillov in *The Possessed*, " all is His
Will, and from His Will, I cannot escape."

ESSENCE is not something divisible, it is oneness, part of the
greater whole—God, pure being in whom essence implies and
also informs existence. Therefore the existent can only try to
become aware through spirit, which is the link between
existence and essence, of the nature of essence, but he cannot
determine it, since it is the very essence that he seeks to know
which creates his existence and conditions his choices. There
cannot be any choice at the level of essence; there is only an
illusion of choices or spurious choices at the level of social life,
social conventions, and words used as social signs. Whatever
is can only be what it is; it is obvious that the possibilities which
came to realisation must have had in them greater vitality than
those which did not come into reality; that vitality is not the
product of will, though will and consciousness, which increase
it, are themselves part of the possibilities which, once they have
been realised, we recognise as forming what we call the true
self. Existence is the only way to know, through actions or
through intuitive apprehensions, what truly is. The realisation
and the revelation of essence through existence is a process
which involves the reduction to oneness of conflicts and
opposites, which have to pass from the realm of possibilities to
the reality of existence.[1] The pre-existence of essence does not
exclude the concept of good and evil, or a form of human
responsibility. Good and evil are related to our awareness or
non-awareness of essence. Not everyone can reach essence,

[1] "The particular has its own interest in world history; it is something finite
and must perish as such. It is this particular which exhausts itself in struggles
with its like, and is partially destroyed. But from the struggle, from the
destruction of the particular, the universal results." (Hegel)

yet everyone is more or less aware of his lack of contact with it, and it is that lack of contact which causes suffering and which alienates from the rest of men, though not from essence, those who embody, as a necessary part of the dialectics of essence, the negative or evil aspects of existence. Essence is amongst other things perfect goodness, that is to say all that fosters in life plenitude, growth of the freedom of the spirit towards perfect harmony. The human being can be vaguely aware of some kind of harmony or of lack of it, and he knows that he might come closer to it by tension towards or attention.[1] This harmony does not imply bliss or lack of tension—something which is only possible at the supra-human level or in timeless moments when all tensions are resolved—but it implies, owing to its nearness to essence, greater vision, greater sensibility and greater capacity for suffering. Existence is one, and therefore individual awareness of essence cannot produce perfect joy; on the contrary, as part of existence, the genius or saint is all the more aware of the distance which lies between the vast body to which he belongs and essence; therefore his suffering is all the greater and reaches the point where the supreme genius, pure essence incarnate—Christ—suffers and dies endlessly for that part of existence which is the negative aspect of essence and which needs to be illumined into positiveness, for, in essence positiveness is all.

The problem of influence, of one cause wilfully and freely determining an effect, does not exist; we only have inextricable and unavoidable relations between the various strands of life, and the poet or the philosopher or any revealers of truth are merely crystals, in quality the same as all other men, in psychic composition closer to the essence, that is to say having a greater awareness of that essence and endowed with varying degrees of luminosity to transmit it. An individual's capacity to cast

[1] Attention not to God, but to something concrete to begin with, and to a wilful emptying of the mind towards a state of pure expectation and nothingness which God might fill with its true reality.

light may be insufficient to reveal by itself the truth, even the truth which is latent in himself, and therefore the light reflected through him by somebody belonging to his own time or to preceding times may help him to see what he could not see through his own means; but the point is that what is illumined, by whatever lights, was already there and had always been there. What an extraneous light can do is not to make the truth, but to help one to delineate the facets of one's individual vision of the truth. Truth is eternal, but it is multifaced or rather apprehended subjectively, and every genuine artist, poet or philosopher can only reveal his own individual aspect of the truth. In order to do that, he has to be truly himself, and he can only be truly himself in moments when he has no self, in states rarely reached and which are the true mark of genius. Poetic knowledge is the inextricable blend of reality with the subjectivity of the poet grasped in a state of spiritualised emotion, something which is akin to Wordsworth's recollected emotion, since it is not the actual emotion but the emotion orientated towards knowledge and creation. In such states, which are the starting moments of creation, the ego or personality is replaced by the creative spirit or genius which is the link with essence. [1]

Essential truth is not invalidated by phenomenal and conceptual changes. A poem containing philosophic notions and concepts which are no longer valid does not *ipso facto* become valueless, if it has some basis of essential truth which transcends historical time. Historical revelation there has been, once and once only, but it had been meant and prepared from the very moment when life began on earth, and therefore, though it is something unique, it is not unconnected with man's previous efforts to transcend reality and the limitations of existence. The search for truth embraces paganism as well as Christianity; the emotions which find their mental representation in concepts appropriate to these two apparently different worlds are linked, and are based on the inherent needs of the human

---

[1] "Poetry is the most philosophic of all writing; its object is truth, not individual and local, but general and operative." (Wordsworth, Preface to Lyrical Ballads).

spirit. Therefore, although the pagan world does no longer fit with the discoveries of modern science, its essential truths, the ontological relationship of things, independent of notional and conceptual representations, are not invalidated by the new concepts. The philosophy, or rather the cosmogony of the *Divine Comedy* may be now invalidated by modern science, but the emotions and the spiritual urgency underlying the poem are not; that is what is important in the search for the perenniality of truth, something which must not be confused with its historicity. In Dante, events and philosophical or religious systems have been purified or washed of scientific truth which has lost its primacy by having been dipped in the poet's creative innocence. It is this kind of innocence which raises poetic creations above good and evil and life's impurities or failings, and confers upon them purity, truth and beauty, qualities which are interchangeable.

Truth is revealed by genius, which is essence becoming being in creations or mental representations apprehensible to the senses or to mind. Genius is not dichotomy or conflict between society and an individual or between conflicting notions; it is the direct expression of essence, therefore oneness, beyond self-hood, and connecting with the realm of 'infinite subjectivity' which is Kierkegaard's description of God. Genius uses conflicts and contradictions to express its own necessity. Wagner's genius, for instance, was, above all, the expression of sadness,[1] hence the choice of his subjects and themes. To try to explain that choice by society or by fortuitous circumstances, is to fail to realise that these phenomenal aspects of life, whose ramifications, links and causalities elude our analysis, are integral parts of an organic whole whose essence

[1] Suffering is always part of genius, for any passage from non-being to being implies suffering, yet suffering which may be transcended into the joy of vision and creation, even if it is the very source or essence of the poetry, as is the case with Leopardi. The joy of creation is the joy hinted at by Coleridge in *Ode to Dejection*. The essence of artistic creation can also be joy, as is the case with Mozart, or with the last cantos of *Il Paradiso* which try to convey the memory of light and the beatific vision which is absolute joy.

genius translates into apprehensible forms. The Heisenberg principle of uncertainty has not been proved to be incompatible with the concept of causation; we are merely taking a leap from our present incomplete knowledge into dogmatic assertion. Our approach to genius should consist above all in attempts to reach, through the analysis of its phenomenal aspects, its essence, and by so doing to increase our consciousness of the true will, and not in attempts to explain it away as the result of social and human conflicts; such explanations are generally based on *a priori* concepts, ideas and beliefs which enable us to exteriorise our 'egos', but not to search for true knowledge, which entails a surrender of the 'ego'. True knowledge obtained through art is not so much explanation and comment as accurate description of phenomenal appearances in view of a possible intuitive grasp of what informs the phenomenon. It is accuracy and intensity of vision in order to go beyond the real into the perennial; it is Cézanne, Vermeer, Rembrandt or Dante. It is 'at-tention' to reality, and not dialectics and attempts to explain causes and ramifications. It is only through intense contemplation of the phenomenon that one might reach an intuitive grasp of its essence; in such cases mind is used more for co-ordination and understanding or penetration of the sense-data than for self-satisfying conjectural flights. To conceive history or existence as a series of might-have-beens, lost tracks or wrong turnings, is to indulge in mental gymnastics as barren as they are meaningless. The words *right* or *wrong*, parts of ethical terminology, ill apply to the processes of life and the universe; they merely exteriorise human points of view which vary with history. They do not attempt to fathom, they merely mark assent or dissent; in the end the conception of artistic and historical movements and changes as willed reactions and influences is the bane of comprehension and the source of unwarranted pride.

A great writer, philosopher or scientist is not 'influenced', that is to say prevailed upon by one of his predecessors or contemporaries to do something which he would not otherwise have done, but he is predetermined by them in the sense that he is inextricably connected with them and prolongs or reacts against them. For instance, Einstein has not been 'influenced' by Clerk Maxwell in the normal use of this word, but he could not have developed his theories without the existence of Clerk Maxwell, who could not have developed his without Lagrange, who could not have developed his without Newton, Descartes, Galileo, etc., back to Pythagoras and to the confines of history. In another way, Bishop Berkeley's subjective idealism is a criticism of Locke and Newton, and also part of Kant's idealism and of what followed via Hume and other predecessors. The list could be extended to range throughout the whole of human history; it is long enough to stress the fact that all these thinkers and scientists are the necessary links in the process of growth of the human mind, and to remind us that any individual revelation of the essential truth is completely out of the realm of influence submitted to will or imitation, approaches which are either spurious or superficial, or confined to the level of social games and fashions and are therefore irreconcilable with the necessary progress of mankind from the particular to the universal.

Artistic conventions or accepted forms are very important in art; they are or they should be in some ways the true expression of things, their 'inscape', originally informed by 'instress' or essence. They may and they do sometimes end in being the whole of art in periods lacking genius and merely filled with craftsmen and technicians, or they may have such a hold on a given period that a genius may have to accept their outward shape and carry them with him as part of his necessity, in the same way as a tree growing in a forest cannot freely take any direction it likes. Such was the case of Racine, who accepted the existing conventions of his age, but fused into them experiences informed with the knowledge which comes, not from the separation of intellect from feelings, or of matter from mind as befitted the age of Descartes, but from the awareness that the two are interrelated and are manifestations of the conflict between finite and infinite which rages in the human being in time, a conflict which, when apprehended by a human consciousness, can be raised beyond time. In contrast with Racine's, Corneille's plays are just like Poussin's paintings, willed constructions, perfect samples of extraordinary rhetoric bearing the imprint of the Cartesian belief that knowledge is a willed act of mind, and that rational man is master of his fate.

Just as all religions, groping through the various stages, from the animistic to the mythical and the spiritual, are part of the human search for God, in the same way all philosophical quests for knowledge are part of the growth of mind which is the unfolding self-consciousness of creation moving towards its source—eternity.[1] This self-consciousness, that is to say this consciousness of the essence, could be called genius,[2] and is something which manifests itself at all levels, individual, national and historical, yet maintaining throughout the same attributes of universality and perenniality. That is to say, genius could appear in what is erroneously described as isolation, though in truth it is not, it is only an optical illusion due to the fact that the very essence of genius is to express and that therefore we only see the expressed and not the hidden or the latent which has gone into the making of the expression. To put it differently, genius could be the most striking growth in a forest composed of similar plants, or it could show external characteristics which distinguish it in space and time in the same way as a palm tree is different from a pine tree or from some prehistoric tree which has ceased to exist, yet fundamentally they are all trees, they share in the same essential quality of being what they are meant to be, which, in the case of genius, at whatever level it operates, is to transcend time by the revelation of essence. That existential revelation is

[1] See Appendix.
[2] In its highest form the saint, who transcends ethnical groups and historical time and is centred upon God and the Incarnation—God's manifestation in life and history.

progressive, and its phenomenal aspect varies according to historical time. The longevity of certain aspects of truth or of certain ideas which embody them varies according to whether they have been given consciousness by Christ, Plato or any other beacon of the human mind bent towards its source.

Although man does not yet know them, there are bound to be laws for the growth and evolution of spiritual matters, in the same way as there are laws for the development of the animal and vegetable world. Human gestation lasts nine months: other animals require less or more time, and have shorter or longer lives than man. Some insects and flowers live only a day or a season, certain trees are said to have lived close on a thousand years. Certain ideas break to the surface of consciousness and fade away within a generation, to reappear perhaps later strengthened with more truth; others take hundreds or thousands of years to grow and still go on growing, spreading out, throwing forth new shoots, dropping off old branches, yet with a stem ever as alive and vigorous as when it broke into time. Ideas break through human consciousness with greater or lesser clarity and they acquire by their emergence into consciousness a greater force, a greater power and speed of growth and therefore a greater impact on their surroundings; then they begin to alter and to become different, and once they have expended their initial force, and groping decay has increased and brought out weaknesses which were merely latent before, they reach a stage when they have to be partially or totally replaced by ever-expanding life. In a forest, the fall of a dead branch automatically releases the growth of another branch or of a growing neighbouring plant which occupies the empty space. So it seems to me with ideas; their weak points leave room for other growths which one day may stifle or overshadow completely the original plant, or they may grow in such a way and reach such proportions that they outgrow their value, and the forest to which they belong has to balance their uselessness with new growths. An idea which has reached maturity becomes the compost which will fecundate and bring forth others. None of the developments of the universe or of life is self-willed, extraneous or due to chance, they are all inextricably bound with previous causes and they express, when they are genuine, essence; it is the same in the spiritual world, part of the universe. An idea is not born as a reaction to another one; the reaction is always there, a latent, integral part of the idea, as darkness is part of light and death part of life. Objectivity is not a reaction to subjectivity, they are only two different ways of looking at the truth. Sometimes, over-self-confident man feels that truth is outside himself and that it can be grasped in its separateness, at other times he feels that he cannot shake himself free from the octopus which is the outside world of which he is a part, and that all he can do is to try to say what it feels like to have this monster all round himself, until the day when he shakes it off or thinks that he has done so, and begins worrying about something else.

The world of the spirit is not the world of the laboratory, the world where one reaction can produce another by the introduction of the required chemicals. What takes place in the world of the spirit is of the order of nature, the order of phenomena like birth, growth and death, phenomena and processes which can be described but not explained, at least not for the moment. Therefore, although collecting data about similarities of forms and ideas may be exhilarating and leisure-filling, it is to my mind only a rather light contribution to the knowledge of any work of art which can rightly lay claims to significance and importance as a revealer of some aspects of the truth. The literary historian can and should confine himself to analysing, without isolating more than necessary, and describing as exactly as possible the various trends, ideas, beliefs and attitudes which seem to prevail in the age and in the individual which engage his attention. A work of art is the expression of an individual sensibility reflecting in concrete form some aspect of the essential truth apprehended through the phenomenal world. The philosopher, the literary historian can describe and give mental coherence to the changing attitudes of man towards the phenomenal and the supra-phenomenal world, and therefore he can give us an admirable idea of the approximate meaning of the terms of reference and of the search of the artist as exteriorised by the work, but he cannot go beyond that without indulging in futile games of superficial data-collecting described as scholarship, or without adopting a positivist attitude and a knowingness which are both alien to art. As for describing its various aspects and similarities and dissimilarities to others, photography will do that well enough.

My first task will be to endeavour to record as faithfully and as exactly as I see them the main changes in man's attitude towards God and nature which range from the ·Renaissance to what is called in literary history 'symbolisme'; these changes, which naturally entail changes in sensibility and therefore in expression, will help us to situate symbolism and to understand something of it. These changes seem to be part of the growth of mind, part of an uninterrupted movement towards a rational explanation of the meaning of life and its relationship to supra-reality and to the universe. That movement, as far as we know, became fully conscious of itself in the sixth and fifth centuries B.C. with Plato and his predecessors and with the great Eastern thinkers who lived at roughly the same time. As far as the Western world is concerned, one could be inclined to agree with A. N. Whitehead that "the safest general characterisation of the European philosophical tradition is that it consists of a series of footnotes to Plato". Symbolisme cannot be understood as a matter of literary influences, it can only be understood as a necessary and unavoidable development of what preceded. Although, as previously suggested, the thought of Plato overshadows the whole of Western civilisation, and although his ideas and those of his predecessor Pythagoras find a wider and wider acceptance in the philosophy, physics and astronomy of our time, it is not necessary to go back 2,500 years to understand symbolism; but it is, I think, necessary to go back to what is accepted as the beginning of the scientific age, or rather to the conscious emergence of a scientific attitude towards life from the seventeenth century onwards. Here I must say that for the sake of brevity, and in spite of the very real risk of distortion through over-simplifications, I must needs confine my remarks to the generally accepted central problem of any work of art—I mean the changing relationship between man and God or transcendence, and between man and the universe, throughout the modern era beginning with Descartes—and to the arts which are, better than any other human actions, an embodiment of these fundamental relationships and of the forces at work in society.

The modern world takes its stand upon the inward drama of the soul. That attitude is not new but is, amongst other things, a development of the importance of the individual personality inherited from the Middle Ages. "The emphasis on the idea of the self, as something primary in experience and providing the basis of an ontology, may be said to be the keynote of modern as contrasted with ancient and medieval philosophy. It was this that Descartes had the merit of being the first to bring into pre-eminence, and thereby, as Whitehead puts it in *Process and Reality*, p. 222, of 'making the greatest philosophical discovery since the age of Plato and Aristotle'."[1]

Descartes expresses the latent thought of his age but not the whole thought of his age, for no epoch is ever homogeneous or without any discordant notes which could be the lingering strains of what preceded or the preliminary sounds of what is to come. Descartes' stand is based upon his ultimate mind and the belief that his consciousness can reach through rational processes the only possible awareness of his own existence and

[1] J. H. Muirhead, *The Platonic Tradition in Anglo-Saxon Philosophy* (Allen & Unwin, 1931), p. 420.

therefore also of the world's existence; this is the first clear step towards subjectivism as against the objective attitude of the ancients, yet it is also a move firmly grounded on the rationalism of the Middle Ages with their faith in an order of things centred upon God, transcendent and immanent to the universe. The trust of the Middle Ages in objects and things, in short in nature as being God's work and a source of joy, a trust which was the foundation of their realistic art, not only continued to exist in the seventeenth century but was a very important ingredient in the scientific attitude. In the mechanistic universe of Descartes, surveyed by the cogitating mind, matter is one thing, spirit is another; they co-exist as the creation of God who has after that retired from it, but they do not interact; there has been transcendence, but on the whole there is no inner grace connecting it with time, and immanence is confined to mind, having less and less need of transcendence and in fact in the end becoming transcendent. In that world, the human body is the prototype of all proportions; humanised nature is a background to man, and both man and nature are examined dispassionately, clinically as spatial matter by the comprehending mind which supplies the subjective content of feelings and the qualities such as colours, sounds, scent, taste, etc., as pertaining to mind.[1] All becomes intellectualised, and this is on the whole the case with seventeenth-century French art, with very few exceptions, the most important being Pascal and, in the theatre, Racine, whose individual genius, permeated by a Christian concept of the world, could sacrifice to the conventions of the age, but whose greatness was such that he could transcend these conventions and give us works informed by the power of the eternal spirit, a power which cannot be apprehended through human will. Yet one must not suggest that Cartesianism suddenly descended upon the Western world and conquered all; far from it; while French and Italian art

---

[1] "By our senses we know nothing of external objects beyond their figure [or situation], magnitude, and motion." Descartes, Sixth Meditation.

was mostly declamatory and rhetorical, Dutch art was still engrossed in the traditions of the Middle Ages, maintaining its delight in the object and its love of exact and minute descriptions. Rembrandt always starts from the real, to rise beyond it towards pure poetry and transcendence; so does Dante; with them, reality becomes transfigured into supra-reality which is its essence. Transcendence is therefore in the 'thisness' of things, existence and creation containing the essence of life for the vision which can descry it. This existential approach to transcendence, essentially Christian, sees in the phenomenal world the form of the essence and knows that it is from time that one apprehends eternity through grace or inspiration, or that it is through life that one reaches truth in the light of God.[1] These were the beliefs of Pascal, a contemporary and co-religionary of Racine. The realism of the Middle Ages, as well as the realism of Dante, Rembrandt, Shakespeare and, at times, of Racine, was a realism through which breaks the glow of a world beyond the real and which is ever tinged with an aura of transcendence, or informed with the mystery of life and the universe which, terminology apart, are the same thing. Underlying the art of the Middle Ages and that of the artists above-mentioned, lies the fact that the subject-object relationship was to all appearances a clear-cut one, I mean by that that reality being considered as the expression of the essence, and form the true expression of feelings, the apprehension of reality or of form took place under the belief that it was an objective experience; the world was God's creation, but it was not God; the work of art was the artist's creation but it was so objectified that it could be accepted on its own individual terms and not through having to try to become the artist.

Descartes discriminated between two species of entities—matter and soul. The essence of matter is spatial extension, the

---

[1] Descartes also believed that his intellect and its discoveries were not alienated from God, but on the contrary informed with God's grace. He said: "Initium Sapientiae Timor Domini", *Œuvres*, ed. Adam-Tannery, 10, p. 8.

essence of soul is cogitation; the two exist without any need of anything else. Such a form of dualism cuts across the whole of life, and the result is that the objective world of science will end in being confined to matter, while the world of philosophy ends in annexing the qualities or the unchanging attributes of matter as forming the subjective content of the cogitating individual mind; the whole of the subject-object experience lies within the mind as one of its private passions, and the intellect is the source of all knowledge divided into psychology and epistemology. The outcome of this attitude of dualism between matter and mind, crystallised in Descartes and there-fore rendered more efficient through the fact that he brought it out from the state of latency in which it was before him, into consciousness, was far-reaching in the arts; it implied a separation between intellect and feelings and a wilfulness (Descartes' *cogito* being reached through will) which is ex-cellent for prose and analytical knowledge but which is necessarily rhetorical and rules out intuitive knowledge, which can only be attained through the unified being in states of selflessness. The result, in the arts, is that we often have form without substance, and intellectual works which are brilliant pieces of dialectics in which sentiments have been turned into sentimentality. We have the rhetorical tragedies of Voltaire, very pale imitations of Racine, with their empty form and their rationalised passions, and we have the melodramatic creations of Diderot and his followers whose plays could easily bring forth floods of tears from their overwhelmed, sentimental audiences. Nothing much can be said about poetry, for in truth there is hardly any until the romantic age.

The eighteenth century is the age of reason, "one-eyed reason deficient in its vision of depth", as A. N. Whitehead puts it,[1] and also the age of sensibilities. It is the age of 'les philosophes' in France, who are no philosophers with the exception of Rousseau, who, like Berkeley in England,

[1] *Process and Reality*, p. 83.

3

sounded a discordant note but did not manage to upset that age of scientific materialism. In the Thomistic theology which dominated the Middle Ages, faith was perfectly at peace with reason; in the eighteenth century the means have become the end, reason has become the object of faith, and the world is a perfect clock wound up for ever and whose key has been thrown into the sea. Time and history, part of time, which before were the means to reach or to deserve eternity, now become the only goals of man living in a world without transcendence and amidst a rationalised nature whose secrets he is about to grasp in order to convert some of them into manna and to bring about the millennium. In that age, the subject-object relationship was in some ways still as clear-cut as before, yet there were already signs that growth was proceeding apace, and that the half-hearted subjectivism of Descartes was developing into the full-fledged subjectivism of Berkeley, Hume and Kant. For Berkeley, Descartes' dualism of mind and reality is fictitious, and it is an attempt to stop half-way at a point which can only be a halt but not an end; for him, there is no reality except that of the mind, and the unity of nature is the unity of ideas in the mind of God. We are in some ways back to Plato with a different terminology. Berkeley contended that what constitutes the realisation of natural entities is the being perceived within the unity of mind; what is thereby realised is the apprehension of things and not the things in themselves. This unity of apprehension defines itself as a *here* and *now*, and the things gathered into the realised unity have essential reference to other places and other times, and are therefore aspects of things grasped into unity by the prehending mind from a standpoint of space and time. Already we have here glimmers of theories which will reappear later under the names of Swedenborg, Schopenhauer and Bradley, and which form the background of the growth of 'symbolisme'

But before we come to them, we should not fail to notice the key position of Kant and how he sought to rectify the balance of the subject-object relationship strongly upset by Berkeley and Hume, by insisting at first on the quasi-objectivity imprinted on the sensory data by the power of understanding and the unconscious synthesis which exists in the apprehending mind. Yet, later, Kant ended with a surrender to the subjectivist principle in stating that the only world which we can know is a construction of the self or ego. Bradley went further and said, "Nothing in the end is real but what is felt, and for me, nothing in the end is real but what I feel."[1] We reach with him the extreme of the subjectivist position, something which, if accepted, renders thought impossible; yet, such was no doubt one of the fundamental beliefs of the romantic attitude. It is an attitude which is instinct with egotism; the individual is all, the world, society, nothing counts but the individual; all life hangs on the individual will. The relationship between subject and object has by now been obliterated, there is no longer an object, there is only the subject. Any experience, any form of knowledge is merely the expression of the individual peculiarities of the subject. The elements perceived by the senses are what counts, the common world of things does not exist, for things are merely attributes of the personality. Historical knowledge, data about things beyond human experience, such as the life of the universe or the meaning of certain non-experienced things, are overlooked because they involve thought. In fact this is the proof that thought had by then outgrown its usefulness and modicum of possible assimilation, so much so that in the perplexed nineteenth century which saw the break-up of a society and the failure of the scientific materialism which animated it, thought was partially rejected.

In German idealism or English romanticism, nature or matter cannot be divorced from its qualities or attributes, and the æsthetic and ethic values of nature arise not from the apprehension of each element in isolation, but, on the contrary,

[1] Quoted by J. H. Muirhead, op. cit., p. 430.

from the basis of an apprehended totality, something in which the brooding presence of the whole informs the various parts. Substance is alive, permeated by the force of the great mind which embraces man and nature and breaks into human consciousness in moments of ecstatic contemplation and unity. St. Paul had said: "When that which is perfect is come, then that which is in part shall be done away";[1] the perfect is God, the 'in part' is the self, the creature; and the perfect comes as the creature puts itself away; sin is the turning of the creature to the 'in part', to itself. Luther, centuries later, added:

> The more we surrender, the more we become perfect.[2]
>
> If one could renounce oneself and perfectly obey, he could be free from sin as Christ was. . . . The more there is of self-ness and me-ness, the more sin, and the less of me, the more of God.[3]
>
> All self love and self-will is sin.[4]
>
> The noble freedom of the will is to work as God's will. . . . In the Kingdom of Heaven there is no own, and anyone seeking his own would go to Hell, and anyone who is without self will rise to Heaven.[5]

Many other Christian thinkers have expressed similar views; what is important here is to note two points: the first is the one which stresses the relationship of the parts to the whole, therefore the organic view of things; the second is the one which insists on the rise to perfection and knowledge through selflessness, which is the way of mystics and also of artists and philosophers from Shakespeare to Schopenhauer or Schelling. The organic view of nature ended in being the view of all romantic poets irrespective of nationality. Wordsworth, the greatest exponent of the brooding presence of nature, felt that in living organisms there was something which science could

[1] I Corinthians, xiii. 10.
[2] Quoted by H. O. Taylor: *Thought and Expression in the Sixteenth Century* (London, 1920), vol. i, p. 196.
[3] Ibid.   [4] Ibid., p. 198.   [5] Ibid.

not grasp, and he always feels that the whole of nature is involved in the tonality of any particular instance. His aim is 'to express the concrete facts of our apprehension of nature which, according to him, are distorted by scientific analysis. He found in nature a refuge against the fleetingness of life, something hugely material he could always turn to in case of fears, worries or doubts. Shelley too loved nature, but in a way different from Wordsworth's; he loved the eternal changefulness of nature, his approach to nature is more ideal-istic in the Berkeleyan or Platonic way; nature is apprehended through the mind, and not at the intuitive, indefinable level of Wordsworth. Shelley was what Wordsworth was not, a worshipper of the mind, of the intellect, and his poetry is permeated by the love of science, source of joy, illumination and human betterment. Yet he did not lose his sense of rever-ence for the mystery of nature and he remained constantly aware of the limitations of the human mind to apprehend the mystery of life and to express it in words.

French romantics do not show anywhere the same sense of mystery towards nature, nor are they capable of the com-munion or ecstatic union with nature which characterises English romantics from Wordsworth and Coleridge to Shelley. There still remains amongst them a good deal of Cartesianism in their attitude to matter and to the apprehension of reality and its expression in words. Nature is for Vigny a stepmother, for Chateaubriand an object of enchantment, and for Lamartine and particularly for Victor Hugo a reservoir of splendid metaphors or a source of mnemonic recollections, but it is never that Wordsworthian vast living organism informed with a spiritual life inextricably bound with that of man. It can no longer be apprehended through mind, but, according to French romantics, it can be felt, and the intellect can still describe these feelings with the accuracy of a language which has slightly altered its terminology but which has the same power, the same mastery over experience as the language of the seventeenth and eighteenth centuries. Only some minor adjustments are apparently needed, and Victor Hugo claimed to have made them. French romanticism caught only the surf of the tidal wave which struck England at the end of the eighteenth century; the force which carried that surf was still too strongly tainted with the scientific materialism of the previous ages; Rousseau, Kant and Hegel had not yet made profound contributions to that current; there were signs of their presence, of course, but they did not come fully to the surface until the last quarter of the nineteenth century. The nature-poetry of English romanticism is a protest against the exclusion of value from the essence of matter, it is above all best characterised by Berkeley's thought which had at last caught up with the exhausted mechanistic materialism of the previous ages. Science had been dethroned, but not by any means done away with, as is proved by the lasting faith in technology; in fact that faith was such that by the second quarter of the nineteenth century science was again in the ascendancy and again threatening to depose the newly reinstated religion.

Kant, more than anybody else, and, later on, Hegel, are the two great thinkers who show better than any others the attempted synthesis between thought and sensory perception, object and subject. It is in Kant that we witness most clearly the attempt at conciliation between the phenomenal world and the mysterious timeless world of Plato which was for Kant not 'idea' but something slightly different, the 'noumenon'. While Kant conceived thoughts as entering into the constitution of objects that we know subjectively and as hiding a beyond, a 'thing-in-itself' which eludes knowledge, Hegel conceives thought as objective and as the absolute universal principle from which all is fashioned. The 'absolute', for Hegel, is not beyond, but *here* and *now*; if we can think truly of the universe, says Hegel, we shall truly have entered into possession of universal life. The 'absolute', so far from being unthinkable, is the object of all thought. Thought can think the infinite because it is itself infinite and the infinite is thought; in the same way, as we shall see later, Mallarmé will throughout his life-dream of enclosing the universe in a book, 'the book' which would end all. Before Hegel, both Fichte and Schelling, the originator of the word 'absolute' in literature, had renounced Kant's unknowable absolute. Fichte had found true reality in the ego and its clear-cut separation from the non-ego, Schelling in the kind of opacity which is neither subject nor object, neither thought nor thing. Hegel had found it in thought, through reason which gives its unity to nature and which will in the end resume it into itself.

By the third quarter of the nineteenth century, the various forces which had caused the buoyancy, the optimism, self-confidence and self-centredness of the first half, had begun to flag. The appetite for experience, the romantic impetus had died down, and the wave of scientific materialism which had been overtaken but not overwhelmed re-emerged with renewed strength. Exuberance and exhibitionism gave way to control, impersonality and to so-called detachment, which are other aspects, no less revealing, of the human personality which entrenches itself behind them so as to play at objectivity. These other aspects merely imply a change of belief, a new set of illusions with the added one that this last illusion is truth. Science and scientific methods are the new illusion, and human behaviour must conform to it; everything must be controlled and measurable, whether it is love or misery; God Himself can only be accepted, on the whole, as a gentleman who knows the rules of accomplished behaviour, as for saints and martyrs, they are bores who do not know how to behave. Yet that world of rosy illusions and comforting pseudo-liberalism was merely a patch in the ever-unfolding scroll. Technology certainly brought about an economic prosperity which could satisfy the middle classes, engrossed in material comfort and dullness, but the spirit was undeniably low. In

France, the methods of the laboratory were transposed to the arts under the names of positivism and naturalism. Reason had regained its illusory mastery, and language could aptly describe reality which was what the mind could apprehend and nothing more; so we had Zola and the Parnassians, and we had Taine who could explain a work of art as one could explain the various samples of flowers or vegetables according to the seed, the ground, the climate, the chemical feedings, etc., etc. Poets and novelists aimed at describing nature or at recording their experience with the same detachment with which Darwin collected and ordered his data for *The Origin of Species*. Gautier, Heredia, Leconte de Lisle painted their pictures with the same objective attitude as Courbet with his firmly-drawn lines and his very definitely set patches of colour; their aim was coherence and clarity without any Rembrandt-like shadows full of mystery; the dangers were fragmented details unrelated to any centre, and superficiality. It was again matter apprehended by the cogitating mind and nothing else, no 'thing-in-itself' as Kant had suggested.

The situation was different in England, where the romantic movement truly marks a profound change in sensibility. Besides that, German idealism, which, together with Berkeley's thought, underlies that movement, was then gaining ground owing to the writings of Coleridge, the translations of Hegel by Hutchison Stirling and others, and the writings of Carlyle. The hold of theology and of positivism was still very strong on British thought, but the need for a form of reconciliation between thought and matter, the ideal and the real, as exemplified by Kant, was widely felt, and the poets of the middle century, like Tennyson and Browning, were torn between these conflicting ideologies, well aware that, although scientific methods applied to the observation of nature were perfectly valid, they could not explain the whole relationship between man and the universe; therefore, although there was full confidence in history and in language to unfold the poetic experience, English poetry never lost completely its sense of mystery. The concentration of the artist upon external appearance or form, even in the case of Flaubert, marks the failure to realise that one cannot reach the essence from the outside through form, and also that beauty is a by-product but cannot be the aim of art which, by so doing, defeats itself and ends in superficiality. The idea is the form, thought Flaubert, echoing German idealism, but he forgot the vital point that the idea is reached not through will and pertinacious searches of external forms, but through a surrender of the will in an act of selflessness which connects time with eternity, and Flaubert was incapable of such a surrender because, as he himself modestly said, he had immense talents but not enough genius:

> Il y a un mot de La Bruyère auquel je me tiens: 'Un bon auteur doit écrire raisonnablement'. C'est là ce que je demande, écrire raisonnablement et c'est déjà bien de l'ambition. Néanmoins il y a une chose triste, c'est de voir combien les grands hommes arrivent aisément à l'effet en dehors de l'Art même. Quoi de plus mal bâti que bien des choses de Rabelais, Cervantès, Molière et d'Hugo? Mais quels coups de poing subits! Quelle puissance dans un seul mot! Nous, il faut entasser l'un sur l'autre un tas de petits cailloux pour faire nos pyramides qui ne vont pas à la centième partie des leurs, lesquelles sont d'un seul bloc. Mais vouloir imiter les procédés de ces génies-là, ce serait se perdre. Ils sont grands, au contraire, parce qu'ils n'ont pas de procédés.[1]

He could achieve, through natural and carefully developed gifts, a certain form of knowledge—clinical or dialectical, but hardly ever bearing the true mark of illumination. He could achieve a certain beauty which bears the imprint of a man of talents, perfect connoisseurship, taste and technical skill, but

[1] Flaubert, *Correspondance* (Conard, Paris, 1926–30), vol. iii, p. 143.

hardly ever that of a man who has seen the burning bush. Flaubert was far too sane, and with regard to Buffon's dictum, he certainly confused patience with pertinacity. Perhaps Buffon himself did not mean anything else, yet patience could have led him to the night of unknowing, while pertinacity only led to exquisite carving and to the polishing up of ideals which he already had in his mind, and which therefore could not be the 'idea', which is beyond individual will. All this to say that genius was not truly there and that the forces which were going to bring new aspects of truth to the surface in France, were not yet strong enough, but they were very close, and signs of their presence were getting more and more numerous.

The very discoveries which the scientific attitude had made possible were carrying with them the seeds of a revulsion towards that attitude, for the new knowledge only proved, and this time decisively, the vastness of the unknown which still surrounded man. It seemed to make clear, at last, the fact that even if we ever came to know what life is, we could never know why there is life, until we ourselves could make it, and for that we should have to be able to begin with the true beginning, which could only be reached by self-creating ourselves at the very start of our process of investigation—an obvious impossibility. Science was by now uncovering secrets which, instead of bolstering up man's pride and self-confidence, were on the contrary reducing him to the Pascalian proportions of the two infinites; instead of being the master of the universe through reason, as in the eighteenth century, or its centre through his will and feelings, as with the romantics, man appeared more and more to be a helpless dwarf deprived of faith in himself and, on the whole, of a transcendental faith which might protect him. In 1859 Darwin published his *Origin of Species*, which made of man, not the centre of the universe, but a mere link in the evolutionary process. The idea that man was not a direct descendant of Adam born some

6,000 years before but, according to Lyell, over 100,000 years old and part of the vast process of creation, was such a shock that many people lost faith not only in religion but also in the unlimited power of science. At the same time the archæological discoveries of Schliemann, Sir Flinders Petrie and Sir Arthur Evans proved that great civilisations such as the Trojan and the Minoan had existed in the past and were not mere legends. These discoveries stimulated the already great interest in history. Tennyson, Browning and the pre-Raphaelites had been, like the romantics, deeply interested in medieval legends. That interest was part of a conscious search for roots in a world stultified and desecrated by abstractions and materialism, and of the desire to escape from the strict conventional morality of the life of their time. *La vie de Jésus* by Renan increased the disquiet; *Das Kapital*, written in 1867, marks the extent of the social unrest and, by transposing Hegelianism to economics, indicates the new trends resulting from the developments of technology.

Scientific materialism, best represented by Descartes and which, for well over two centuries, with the exception of Spinoza and Leibnitz, had dominated Western thought, had reached its final maturity and was breaking up under the weight of its own fruits—epistemology and psychology. Scientific investigation, supporting philosophers' views, had proved that the world was, in every respect, one. "Physicists tell us that nothing is isolated, everything makes reference to everything else, every event by reason of its very nature requires the whole universe in order to be itself." These are not the words of symbolist poets, but of J. W. N. Sullivan in *The Basis of Modern Science*.[1] "If there is anything to which modern thought is everywhere coming it is this conception of a wholeness. . . when biologists are everywhere disowning the dualism between organic and inorganic in the interest of a deeper unity and continuity between them, we may be justified in feeling

[1] 1928, p. 240.

that an old dream of philosophy is coming to have a new meaning through the observations of the laboratory", says J. H. Muirhead,[1] and on the same page he quotes J. S. Haldane as having said in his Gifford lectures that "surrounding nature is not an influence outside our lives but within them". Descartes had discriminated between two species of entities—matter and soul, the essence of matter being spatial extension, the essence of soul being cogitation; by the last quarter of the nineteenth century it has become clear, as it had been clear to Kant much earlier, that owing to such a division the very reality of things could not even be hinted at. With Bergson emerges the organic conception of physiological science and a repudiation of the abstract Newtonian conception of nature which for him, as for the romantics, is organic. His distinction between time and duration, his insistence on the continuous presence of the past, together with the exploration of the subconscious by Freud, complete the picture.

Descartes' world has truly come to an end, and with it a long period of mental certitudes. The phenomenal world is no longer looked upon as matter confined to space and time, it is alive, it is an integral part of life, and the relationship between matter and spirit has become as inextricable as that of mass and energy; in fact the whole of life is now accepted as movement. Later, with William James' famous book *Does Consciousness Exist?*, published in 1904, and crystallising thoughts in process of development, we have what is perhaps the most important challenge to the foundation of Cartesian knowledge—consciousness or the ego. Consciousness, Descartes' ego, the basis of his awareness of existence, is now found to be completely indefinable in its constant flow. What is consciousness?—the awareness of something, that something which is held and makes consciousness, just as music is the sound heard or unheard; but there are all kinds of music, as there are all sorts of aspects of consciousness, yet the certitude has come that there

[1] Op. cit., p. 434.

is, not one single ego which remains the centre of consciousness, but only one permanency—the continuous movement from non-being to being. Therefore time past and time future only exist in the moment of apprehension which brings them to life in the present. Time does not die, time is memory brought to life in the moment of intense consciousness which redeems time and discovers its true identity. Cartesian time was sequential, now there is only the present and, for those who believe in it, eternity; those who do not can call it non-being. All things are simultaneous, and can be brought to life in the instant of intensity which is the moment of consciousness—the aim of art. The time of Bergson is a time in which the present contains all time. This concept is by no means new; as in most things, Plato had already something to say on that problem, in the *Timaeus* we read:

> Wherefore He [the Father] planned to make a movable image of Eternity, and, as He set in order the Heaven, of that Eternity which abides in unity He made an eternal image moving according to number, even that which we have named Time. For simultaneously with the construction of the Heaven, He contrived the production of days and nights and months and years which existed not before the Heaven came into being. And these are all portions of Time, even as 'was' and 'shall be' are generated forms of Time, although we apply them wrongly without noticing to Eternal Being. For we say that it 'is' or 'was' or 'will be', whereas in truth of speech 'is' alone is the appropriate term; 'was' and 'will be', on the other hand, are terms properly applicable to the Becoming which proceeds in Time, since both of these are motions.[1]

Eternity is the 'thing-in-itself' or the Idea, the only thing that truly *is*, an ever changeless, complete, single act in an eternal present. Time and existence are the becoming of eternity

[1] Plato, *Timæus*, *Works*, edited by R. G. Bury, vol. vii, p. 77.

whence they proceed and progressively reveal. The Christian concept of time is very close to that of Plato; according to it, time and eternity are connected by the act of grace—the instant which lifts time to eternity; the instant is individual and existential; the apprehension of eternity can only be from time and the perceptual world and through an individual self which in these moments, becomes self-less. In Hegel's objective idealism, true reality, beyond space and time, is one single, closed whole; but this closedness is obtained through mind working through universal apperception, denying or forgetting its finitude as part of the phenomenal world. Thought might think the infinite but it certainly cannot prehend it except at the point where it ceases to be thought and becomes reality—a point which can only be attained by starting from time clearly differentiated from eternity. In our age, the Christian concept of time is still the same; the time of Einstein is also two-dimensional; in a recent interview to the American press he has said that man looks on individual existence as a sort of prison and that he wants to experience the universe as a single significant whole. He himself has devoted all his energy to the search for the equation which could embody the laws of the universe and could therefore make possible this kind of experience for those who could grasp its meaning.

These remarks point to the fact that by the last quarter of the nineteenth century the idea of a new relationship between man and the universe, an idea whose development can be traced as far back as Plato and Pythagoras, had become part of the clear consciousness of the arts, instead of the vague implicitness which it had assumed previously with English romanticism. The gist of this idea is that the mind cannot apprehend reality separated from it, but can only apprehend its phenomenal aspects in an experience which unites subject and object, and involves the unified sensibility of the subject; that means that the artistic experience which, in the Cartesian world of knowledge through mind, could be grasped and described in its entirety, here becomes on the contrary a process of discovery, an adventure which, lacking the *a priori* concepts upon which to stand, is a journey towards the unknown in search of something—the 'thing-in-itself' or the inner reality which can be hinted at but can never be discovered. The whole excitement is in the journey, and for the writer the media employed are the words, but this time not used in order to clothe concepts whether purely mental or emotional, but as a means to try to suggest, through all their aspects representing the whole being involved in the process, the imaginative graph of the experience which the artist lived in the course of his journey to knowledge. Since knowledge is no longer an act of the cogitating mind centralising and therefore intellectualising all sensory processes, but an apprehension through senses and mind of the phenomenal aspects of a hidden reality, the senses and the mind are both fully and organically engaged in the attempt to register the fleeting reactions of a subject making progressive contacts with an object or with the outside world. That is why the various sensuous aspects of language—the musical and the pictorial, together with rhythm and logical meaning—are all involved in a new formula based on the attempt, not to describe, but to suggest or to register the moving tension towards an ever-receding core. "Creation", as Collingwood said, "is the act of imagination; an artist paints or writes to help himself to discover what he imagines, what he tries to see with his imagination. Art for the creative mind lives in the mind, its interest is there, not on canvas or paper." The work of art, as Kant said, has no purpose, it is merely purposive. The whole work of art does not exist in the mind of the artist, it comes into existence by experimenting with the parts; the poet proceeds not from idea to expression but from expression to idea—source. Art is the realisation of the individuality of the artist through progressive self-discovery in action, without preconceived ideal or set purpose—social, religious or otherwise; and least of all is it Art for Art's sake; it is obeying one's inner laws, the laws the individual was made for, which are to reveal his own aspect of truth, part of the great Truth. Knowledge is no longer subjective intellectualism, that is to say the work of an all-powerful ego which draws to itself as a magnet the elements of static materiality, but on the contrary receptivity, enquiry, tension towards some elusive unknowable reality which the devout might reach through grace and the mystic in acts of complete surrender which are the foundations of true knowledge. Knowledge is consciousness, the true aim of poetry, but consciousness in our time is no longer a Cartesian entity, but a kind of Bergsonian continuous becoming. What Descartes called the 'Je', now only is and knows itself in the act of consciousness, and the rest of the time it remains, as Husserl put it, 'in parenthesis'. Consciousness is not a concept or a starting point as Boileau suggested, but an end, the goal of the journey from non-being and darkness to being and light. 'Le rêve' of Baudelaire or Valéry is not the subconscious of Freud and the surrealists, but on the contrary a state in which mental and perceptual activities take place not according to a willed conceptual pattern, but as a growth whose strength and range vary according to genius, towards consciousness and knowledge. Consciousness, the inextricable combination of experience and awareness of experience, breaks gently like dawn from darkness, then it increases in strength, penetrates underwoods and deep valleys, until it finally illuminates mountains and sky in the glory of the day—which is the completed work or poem.

These views of knowledge illumine all the theorising of the symbolist movement; one can easily understand how the words, used like Tom Thumb's pebbles in his journey through the wood of memory or the past, will be arrayed according to their capacity to suggest this very fleeting experience, and not as a firm receptacle of an already existing core; they will be essentially transient and fleeting, and their symbolic value, I mean their referential value to logical meaning, will be reduced to the minimum. They will be, as much as words can stand it, what they are in themselves, the organic notations of an experience. In two respects, in respect of fleetingness and transience, and in respect of being essentially themselves, they resemble musical notes, which, at best, should be what they are and nothing else. The new way of presenting the poetic experience also resembles music in the fact that structural rhythm plays an essential part in suggesting the poetic experience and the emotion which underlies it. We shall see later how a good deal of Mallarmé's insistence on poetry as music, which was taken by many as being the result of Wagner's influence, was in reality due to the very nature of the poetic experience which, in its fluidity, had drawn nearer to music. Life in all its aspects, from the most minute to the cosmological level, from the most static matter to feelings and all aspects of the human psyche, is now conceived as movement and timelessness. The novel, based on sequential time, has its last great representative in Flaubert; after him Gide, Proust, Joyce concerned themselves not with telling stories conveying through characters a criticism of the society to which these characters belonged, but rather aimed at conveying the moment of present experience and intensity which, whether it embraces twenty-four hours or two-score of years, brings together the simultaneity of events which form the duration of a human consciousness. Whitehead describes that moment as the "creativity of the world which is the throbbing emotion of the past hurling itself into a new transcendent fact". It is the search for time lost and time regained of Proust, it is the abolition of time and matter of Dostoevski and the moment of dénouement of Gide. *L'Après-midi d'un Faune*, *La Jeune Parque*, *Ulysses*, and, later on, *Four Quartets*, are above all the records of journeys of discoveries across various *états-d'âme*; centred round a story, as is the case with *Ulysses* and *L'Après-midi d'un Faune*, a myth in the case of Valéry, and concrete experiences in the case of Eliot, with whom the structure of the poem approximates most to the structure of a musical composition.

We have examined previously the distant roots and various stages towards what Whitehead describes as the revolution in metaphysics which fully emerged during the last quarter of the nineteenth century and is known in the arts as symbolisme. We have seen how art, as well as life, is a question of continuous growth, excluding the concept of fathers, yet not the concept of light as consciousness and as a means of quickening the process of growth. We have seen that there is nothing more erroneous than the concept of literature as a succession of movements started by various individuals; we shall see now the untenability of the idea of a literary movement as being something either homogeneous or caused by one single writer or more. The father of symbolisme is supposed to be, according to certain critics, Edgar Allan Poe, and after him came Baudelaire and a whole progeny which ranges from Verlaine to Mallarmé. We have already examined the evidence of the distant roots of the attitude to art known as symbolisme we shall come closer to it yet, and examine the elements which enter into it and the principal names associated with them; then an examination of the main tenets of symbolisme will make clear its heterogeneity and the distance which separates Mallarmé from Rimbaud, Baudelaire and Poe, or from the small fry—flag-wavers, and spurious imitators who claimed to support but rather distorted the views of their idols. In the course of this examination we shall easily realise the impossibility of establishing a body of positive beliefs applicable to all the writers of this movement, and therefore the necessity, if one does not want to distort the truth any more than can be avoided, of confining oneself to a few negative beliefs to which they could all subscribe and which, in the end, amount to nothing more than a common attitude to art.

The true poet, as well as the truly great philosopher, can sense the latent forces of his age and bring them to light; each one will use his own means, the poet will concentrate on imaginative truth and the philosopher on logical truth, though there are points where logic falls short of the truth while imagination can at least, through metaphor or symbols, hint at it, so that the philosopher has to be what he is when he is truly great—a poet. Besides that, poets and philosophers need one another's support to strengthen their faith in the truth which they hope to have discovered. The philosopher finds in the poet's work the concrete evidence which is lacking in his abstractions; the poet finds in the philosopher the logical, rational confirmation of aspects of the truth which he had intuited; in all cases of greatness these two aspects of mind— the philosophical and the poetic—are in varying degrees part of the same person—Plato, Coleridge, Goethe, Wordsworth, Rousseau, etc. Baudelaire, Mallarmé and Valéry found in the German idealists support for their views; their views were not derived from them, but confirmed by them, as G. M. Hopkins' views were confirmed by his reading of Duns Scotus. Poets had long felt with Kant that the 'thing-in-itself' could never be apprehended but only hinted at. The famous theory of the oneness of the universe apprehended in moments of mystical union with the great one is as old as Plotinus and, again, is only a derivation of Plato's beliefs. It is also Schelling's theory, it fits with the Kantian theory of the 'noumenon', and it was quite widespread in England and in France too, through the writings of Carlyle, Victor Cousin, Taine and others. Carlyle had said: "The universe is but a vast symbol of God; nay, if thou wilt have it, what is man himself but a symbol of God?"[1] These views are those of Swedenborg, Boehme, Blake and many others, and these names are only mentioned to stress the fact that the mystic and idealistic approach to literature was gaining ground and tended more and more to see in art, not communication of information, but the source of strong emotional experiences and a revelation of the mystery of cre-

[1] *Sartor Resartus* (Walter Scott, London, 1888), book III, chapter iii, p. 198.

ation. Kant had already been in some ways a mediator between Descartes and Berkeley, and Descartes and Plato; Schopenhauer is the mediator or the linch-pin between Plato and Kant; with him the apprehension of the Platonic Idea by a mind free from the will, that is to say in the Kantian condition of 'disinterestedness', becomes the foundation of art. Here one cannot help thinking of Keats' genius and his awareness of this necessity which he called 'negative capability'. Schopenhauer's belief coincides with that of Schelling which, through Kant, goes back to Berkeley and further, and which is that when one is lifted by the spirit, the separation between subject and object vanishes from consciousness in a state of perfect æsthetic exaltation which is a transcendental moment. Plato held that the *Idea*, which, as Schopenhauer has shown, is the Kantian 'thing-in-itself', can be known through the abstracting power of the intellect. The sensuous aspects of an object are subject to physical laws and perishable, but the intellect can abstract from these sensuous perceptions an absolute beauty, the idea of beauty, transformed into eternity, and freed from *le hasard*, as Mallarmé, in his quest for Platonic Beauty of Idea, would have put it. Kant showed that what was regarded, in the case of Descartes, as an object of knowledge was in reality only a mode of knowledge, space, time, causality being not the qualities of the thing perceived, but forms present in the mind at the time of the experience; therefore what we know is not the real object, but the object of the mind, that is to say reality seen as an object of sense. The abstracting intellect of Plato could get rid of causalities but not of the thinking subject and perceived object, therefore he could not reach a primary experience of being; though the neo-Platonists could, but only by a surrender of the intellect. Schopenhauer, Schelling and the romantics, especially Wordsworth and Coleridge, saw the solution in a complete fusion of the subject-object relation.

> Are not the mountains, waves and skies, a part
> Of me and of my soul, as I of them?

says Byron; and this is what Schopenhauer says:

> . . . whatever the object is, be it a landscape, a tree, a
> rock, a building, when, to use a pregnant German phrase,
> we *lose* ourselves entirely in this object, forgetting our
> individuality, our Will, and only continue to exist as the
> pure subject, the clear mirror of the object, so that it is as
> if the object alone were there, without anyone to perceive
> it, and one can no longer separate the perceiver from the
> perception, but both have become one because the whole
> of consciousness is filled and occupied with one single
> sensuous picture; if then the object has to such an extent
> passed out of all relation to something outside it, and the
> subject out of all relation to the will, then that which is so
> known is no longer the particular thing as such but it is
> the *Idea*, the eternal form, the immediate objectivity of the
> will at this grade; and therefore, he who is sunk in this per-
> ception is no longer individual, for in such perception the
> individual has lost himself; but he is pure, will-less, pain-
> less, timeless subject of knowledge.[1]

Plato's thought would hardly have repudiated such conclusions,
as is proved by certain passages of the seventh epistle; above all,
Christian thinkers, Protestant or Catholic, have stressed the
profound necessity 'to die in order to live': "When the soul
is steadfast in an overcoming of herself and passes into a not-
herself, then is she through grace. This is the highest office of
grace that it brings the soul to the true self. Grace robs the soul
of her works, grace robs the soul of her own existence"
(Eckhart).[2] Whether for religion or for art, the way to truth
is the same—through a complete surrender of the will.

"Art", says Schopenhauer, "renders the eternal Ideas which

[1] A. Schopenhauer, 'The World as Will and Idea; the Platonic idea, the
object of art', *Works* (translated by Haldane and Kemp, Trübner & Co.,
London, 1883), vol. i, p. 231.
[2] H. O. Taylor, *Thought and Expression in the Sixteenth Century* (London,
1920), vol. i, p. 194.

have been apprehended in pure contemplation, that which is substantial and abiding in all the phenomena of the world; and becomes, according to the material in which it renders them, plastic art, poetry or music. And the essential character of genius consists precisely in the exceptional capacity for this contemplation."[1] The idea—object of art—is certainly the Platonic Idea; besides that, let us note that, like Plato, Schopenhauer gives pre-eminence to music as the highest of the arts and as showing true reality directly and not through the objects of the senses as in the other arts; in fact, one cannot but be led to ask whether, in the last resort, true reality is not music, the music unheard of course, which was the Idea of Plato.

Here we have the concern for music which underlies symbolisme and the attempt to reach the idea which characterises Mallarmé but certainly not Baudelaire or Rimbaud. Baudelaire's and Rimbaud's views lean heavily on the notion of an enchanted Eden-like world, the world of innocence of Rousseau, the lost childhood to be glimpsed at by the inspired artist who tries to recapture it through his art. Neither of them denies the existence of the phenomenal world; they start from it in their quest for paradise. The problem is different with Mallarmé; in his case the poet is the creation, projected out of the phenomenal world which has been annihilated, in order to reach the idea—the absolute; all that remains of the phenomenal world is its mental image which can summon the unchanging qualities, in short the abstracted, essentialised aspects rising towards the idea. In some ways this is closer to Berkeley than to Schopenhauer,[2] who differentiates clearly ideas from concepts, while Mallarmé, annihilating by a mental process matter located in space and time, concentrates on values mostly affective in order to reach towards the idea. For Baudelaire, the translator of Poe, the herald of Wagner in France, the

---

[1] A. Schopenhauer, op. cit., pp. 239–40.
[2] The wilful abstracting process of Mallarmé is still Cartesian, while the *Idea* of Schopenhauer is reached in moments of will-less contemplation.

appointed founder of symbolism and the author of 'corre-spondances', all things are symbols of a transcendental reality which suffuses nature, and the artist is the priest of 'le beau et l'idéal', if he has the gift to read the signs and to render the invisible apprehensible to the senses. None of these beliefs was new, and most of them had already a very long history behind them. The interrelationship of the senses, the conception of the phenomenal world as a reflection of the ideal are old indeed, they are creeds which involve such names, to quote only a few, as Plato, Plotinus, Berkeley and Swedenborg, the great admiration of Balzac, who was the great admiration of Baudelaire. As for 'audition colorée' or Baudelaire's views on 'correspondances', they were part of the stock-in-trade of later romantic poets. Symbols are part of the phenomenal world, they are anything present to any of the senses, and the artist notes their cross-references between the different senses and their reflections from a world beyond the senses: "C'est cet admirable, cet immortel instinct du beau qui leur fait considérer la terre et ses spectacles comme un aspect des correspondances du ciel."[1] Art is mediation by genius which reveals what truly is. This point of view, which is that of Baudelaire and Rimbaud, was, we have seen, previously the point of view of German idealists, and of their greatest British exponent, Carlyle, who said:

> Another matter it is, however, when your symbol has intrinsic meaning, and is of itself fit that men should unite around it. Let but the God-like manifest itself to sense; let eternity look more or less visibly through the sense-figure. . . . For is not a symbol ever, to him who has eyes for it, some dimmer or clearer revelation of the God-like? . . . Of this latter sort are all these works of art; in them (if thou know a work of art from a daub of artifice) wilt thou discern eternity looking through time; the God-like rendered visible [3]

[1] Baudelaire, *Art Romantique*, p. 159.   [3] Op. cit., p. 201.

[2] "Il y a bien longtemps que je dis que le poëte est l'intelligence par excellence et que l'imagination est la plus scientifique desfacultés par ce que seule elle comprend l'*analogie universelle*; ou ce qu'une religion mystique appelle la correspondance." (Baudelaire Cor. Gen. I. p. 367).

The bridge between time and eternity is the work of art, the expression of genius. Both Baudelaire and Rimbaud would have subscribed to this attitude, but not Mallarmé, who did not aim at revealing the hidden reality but at replacing the phenomenal world—*le hasard*—by its mental picture tending towards the Idea.

For the whole symbolist movement, as well as for the æsthetic movement, Mallarmé excepted, art was a religion and the poet was the priest revealing the mystery of life. Every element of life and nature is covered by the law of *correspondances*; therefore every fitting metaphor which arouses a response is necessarily a *correspondance*;[1] the poet is the one who has the gift of pointing out analogies and of finding the exact and truly alive metaphors; the greater the poet, the wider his range of apprehension in space and time and also the greater the fitness and force of his metaphors. But for the whole of them, continuing in some ways the tradition of Wordsworth and Coleridge, the phenomenal world was the starting point and the foundation of their metaphors and analogies; not so for Mallarmé; he was all in one, the priest without temple who has projected all and himself in his song, in his music, rising from nowhere to nowhere; he has become God. Looking at him on the plane of literary history, one might be tempted to say that he was in some ways one of the developments towards a dead end of this religion of art. Baudelaire did not insist on magic and on art as a means of revealing the mystery of life through language, he insisted more on the singularity of the poet as 'l'être maudit', the crucified whose blood would illumine the face of the world; Rimbaud is bolder, more impatient with reality whose secret he wants to force as a 'voleur de feu'. He is the possessed, the demiurgic force, self-conscious of his gifts and of the magic or caballistic value of the words to reveal the mystery; he thought he could be an angel, the proudest of the angels—Lucifer, capable of wrenching God's secrets. But Mallarmé quietly behaved as if he were

[1] "With the good poets, comparison, metaphors and epithets come from the inextensible ground of the universal analogy and cannot come from anywhere else" (Baudelaire).

God, at least he provided himself very modestly with most of God's attributes, the most important being the power of self-creation, that is to say of being the source of his own transcendence.

We can see by these contrasts between its three main representatives alone, how impossible it is to advance a theory of symbolism which could do justice to the whole movement. The terms 'literary symbol' and 'symbolisme' are terms which were introduced by what seem to be accidents,[1] and are too elusive to make a satisfactory definition possible. They are terms which are only useful as clusters of meanings containing various disparate elements ranging from profound philosophical changes to notions of mysticism and mere attitudinising. Nevertheless, in the field of literary history the word 'symbolisme' suggests certain connotations just as definite as other similarly vague words like 'romanticism' or 'aestheticism'. It suggests, as previously indicated, certain predominant attitudes to reality and language which came to clear consciousness in the last quarter of the nineteenth century and have shown prolongations in our time. It stands for the belief in a world of ideal beauty and the conviction that it can be realised through art. Symbolisme is, by and large, a kind of religion requiring the undivided attention and the full devotion of its worshippers. The symbols are not church symbols with their centuries-old connections and well-established meanings. On the contrary, they vary according to the poet. Generally speaking, one could define these symbols as a form of indirect, metaphorical speech meant to carry or to suggest a hidden reality. Therefore anything, phenomenon or trait, which bears witness to the supernatural or universal analogy in the world, any sign which tradition has invested with a supernatural meaning or powerful emotional resonance, any allegory, any myth, fable or legend or poetic image indicative of the poet's mental and affective preoccupations, is used as a symbol, a

---

[1] See note at the end of this chapter.

47

correspondence or a means of suggestion. This is indeed a fluid and rather all-embracing definition in which we might find something for every symbolist, but which easily breaks down as soon as we examine the doctrines of the various writers who were supposed to be part of the movement. "Le symbole a pour caractère essentiel d'éclore spontanément, sans réflection, sans analyse dans une âme simple qui ne distingue même pas entre les apparences matérielles et leurs significations réelles."[1]

This form of Berkeleyan idealism might at a pinch apply to Verlaine in search of fluidity and vague emotions seized in their swift transitions as fleeting as musical notes; it might apply to Maeterlinck; it will not apply to Baudelaire or to Rimbaud, who were not 'des âmes simples', and it is certainly the anti-thesis of Mallarmé's or of Valéry's æsthetics. To seize the spontaneity, the fleetingness of poetic images and therefore of poetic truth is to a certain extent the aim of Baudelaire, and in a lesser degree of Rimbaud, but Mallarmé and Valéry, with their insistence on consciousness and remoteness from dream, were at the opposite of such attitudes of daydreaming and receptivity. On this score they were rather at one with Poe and his insistence on composition. Yet one must not go too far; Baudelaire was an extremely conscious artist, for him daydreaming did not mean going to sleep, it meant on the contrary staying awake, working hard, composing poetry. Dream is in fact the result of consciousness, of imagination operating from the phenomenal world and very controlled in its flights which end in construction.

> Architecte de mes féeries
> je faisais à ma volonté
> sous un tunnel de pierreries
> passer un océan dompté.[2]
>
> (*Rêve Parisien*)

---

[1] Péllissier, *Revue des Revues*, 15 March 1901.
[2] *Les Fleurs du Mal*, edited by Barnard (London, 1924), p. 174.

To control 'un océan dompté' is obviously no act of passivity. Even Nerval, who advocated so repeatedly the value of dream for literature, does not fail to advocate control in order to build the work of art. And Rimbaud, 'le voyant', the apostle of the value of the subconscious as a source of art, never confused art with surrender of control. It was he who said, "le poète se fait voyant par un dérèglement de tous les sens", but *se fait* is an act of will, and the *dérèglement* has to be maintained and its results noted. Besides that, he is much more explicit in his famous letter to Démeney, written on 15 May 1871, where he says: "Je est un autre, . . . cela m'est évident, j'assiste à l'éclosion de ma pensée: je la regarde, je l'écoute." It is false to say, "I think", says Rimbaud; one should say, "one thinks me". This is a form of reaching true knowledge which is shared by Nietzsche as well as by Christian thinkers and mystics. The true poet has no *I*; it is only by reaching the state of not-self that he can discover the universal language which sums up creation and communicates essence to individual existence. Rimbaud felt that if he could destroy the shell of the ego and personality he would reach the true objectivity of the unchanging self. In order to be *voyant* the poet must first know himself, so that he may tend more and more towards those states of pure self or knowledge when he is nothing more than the tension towards, or an expectation for words which will tell of the mystery which he could not normally apprehend. The poet's existence is a constant preparation for such moments: "La première étude de l'homme qui veut être poète est sa propre connaissance entière, il cherche son âme, il l'inspecte, il la tente, il l'apprend."[1] This implies self-attention, devotion to experience, and conscious effort. Rimbaud is above all concerned with experience, prepared to do anything to reach the unknown, ready for any sacrifice to know the truth; in fact he is both Christ and Satan at the same time, he is the

[1] Lettre à Démeney, 15 May 1871, first published by Paterne Bérrichon in *La Nouvelle Revue Française*, October 1912.

symbol of pride—"le grand criminel, le grand maudit"—but he is also the scapegoat, tortured for the sake of the knowledge and the wisdom which he wishes to give to men. But none of his searches is a repudiation of control, but rather an attempt to extend "l'état de rêve" to the waking life: "Je m'habituai à l'hallucination simple; je voyais une mosquée à la place d'une usine" (*Délire, Alchimie du Verbe*). For him, the one who is richest in dream is the greatest poet; yet he overlooks one important fact, which is that for the poet the problem is not only to have the dream or the vision, but to record them or to see them in words, for they are nothing until they have coalesced into words.

Poe's 'symbolism', with its stress on atmosphere, was in some ways in the tradition of English romanticism—in some ways only, for Poe's processes were too intellectual and artificial in comparison with the visionary power and the sweep and movement of the poetry of the great English romantics. It seems to me that, in a minor way, Verlaine is nearer these poets than any other poet, including Poe. He was the poet of fleeting suggestions and changing emotional states, and he conveys these imprecise states in precise rhythms and sensuous images; in brief, in perceptions which carry the wealth of imaginative life and enlarge the meaning of the real. His images are not static, they are dynamic, but they are extremely sensuous and they bear the mark of the tension which gives each instant its timeless duration. The poetic process was something natural to Verlaine; practically everything he touched became poetry; his endeavours to reach fleetingness in art are part of the Bergsonian stream of consciousness; he too knew that the true reality of things, part of the mystery, could only be hinted at. With Poe, vagueness is not a sensation, but a technique wilfully adopted in order to convey, through rhythm, effects alien to the words, which he used for their sound. Poe's words are used as by the Parnassians, and later by the imagists; they are precious jewels whose sound or pictorial value aims at achieving an effect—the creation of an atmosphere. It is not the same with Mallarmé. He too, like Poe and Verlaine, was concerned with imprecision and vagueness, but his was a mathematical and willed imprecision, that is to say the greatest precision; the words were used as signs or symbols, yet not for their sound value only, as is often the case with Poe, for Mallarmé aims at creating not an experience but an absence or hollow of experience: "à l'égal de créer: la notion d'un objet, échappant, qui fait défaut".[1] The imprecision of Verlaine is imprecision of feelings and synæsthesia, an interpenetration of the senses conveying an effect of oneness; that of Poe is merely sonorous imprecision; the poet does not have a vision or an imaginative grasp of the experience owing to an incapacity to focus it; he only remains as a kind of echoing centre. In the end Mallarmé lost himself in obscurity, Verlaine in loose writing, and Poe in cymbalism.

In the foregoing pages I have insisted on the longevity and the range of the growth of the literary phenomenon known as symbolism, and on the singularity of its most important members. It might not be without interest to conclude with a few remarks on some general beliefs or attitudes common to all. The romantics had sought experience for its own sake, because the will only knows itself in action; romanticism is the apologia of the individual will and of the naked sensibility, and the romantic writer had tried to test all the possibilities of life— love, travel, politics, etc. For the symbolist, all this exploration of life was vain, the only possible field of exploration was art or dream, the rest was vulgar, below the poet's dignity, for his field of activity ought to be imagination and, in the end, non-being. The romantic despised society, the symbolist ignores it as being part of a reality which, with its transiency and vulgar agitations, is not worth the thought of the poet or of the symbolist hero.

[1] Mallarmé, *Œuvres Complètes* (Gallimard, 1947), p. 647.

What has the Earth ever realised, that drop of frozen mud, whose Time is only a lie in the heavens? It is the Earth, dost thou not see? which has now become the illusion! Admit, Sara: we have destroyed, in our strange hearts, the love of life—and it is in REALITY indeed that ourselves have become our souls. To consent, after this, to live would be but sacrilege against ourselves. Live? our servants will do that for us. . . . Oh, the external world! Let us not be made dupes by the old slave, chained to our feet in broad daylight, who promises us the keys to a palace of enchantments when he clutches only a handful of ashes in his clenched black fist![1]

says Axël, Villiers de l'Isle-Adam's hero, to his beloved Sara. That attitude is in varying degrees that of most symbolist writers. It underlies a good deal of Baudelaire's and Rimbaud's reactions, though in the end Rimbaud probably felt the futility of his demiurgic attempts and opted for humility and the grossness and also the reality of life. It is part of the texture of Laforgue's Lohengrin, of Mallarmé's Igitur, or of Valéry's Monsieur Teste, yet in the middle of his life, Valéry too decided that "le vent se lève, il faut tenter de vivre", and later on Yeats came to the same conclusions. The romantics had despised the bourgeois, symbol of growing materialism; by the end of the century it had become useless to despise the all-powerful bourgeois, the only thing the writer could do was to ignore him, and with him society; gone were Rousseau's, Shelley's or Lamartine's dreams of bringing men back to the lost Eden, it was either the ivory tower, the desert, or the private world of absinthe-inspired dreams. Politics and social preoccupations, which were part of the romantic poet's mind, were found to be completely alien to the serene refined vision of the symbolist artist. His was the poetry of the inner

[1] Translated by Edmund Wilson, op. cit., pp. 262–3.

world, and of experiences singular and with an uncommunicable core of truth. But it was also a poetry shorn of attitudinising, which was useless since the mob and society were of no importance; it was a poetry of refinement and taste, the product of personalities extremely conscious of their exalted or preordained duty to art, and practising their worship of beauty with uncompromising devotion. If the world of the symbolist artist was narrow, if the air which surrounded it was rarified, it also was singularly controlled, dignified in its rigid devotion to ideals self-consciously, painfully sought. Here was no attempt to please the mob, preach a creed or cater for applause; the artist could, like Mallarmé or Proust, live his life secluded in his cork-lined room or in his private world of the imagination, but there was no compromise with triteness or a slapdash method of expression as had been the case with artists preoccupied first and foremost with their message. For the symbolist writer, form was all, and form was only the veil of the unseizable reality whose core was not the will-centred 'ego' of the romantics but the uncommunicable self or the 'thing-in-itself' of Kant. The 'thing-in-itself' of Kant or the 'thisness' or instress of Hopkins is the essential reality of things related to the great truth, and their inscape, their phenomenal shape is informed with the inner truth, which only of genius or the saint can reach and does reach directly through his own means. Hopkins, for instance, had not been to Paris, nor had he read any theories of symbolism, yet nobody practises synæsthesia more naturally than he does; in fact, in the whole poetry of the Western world there seems to be nothing quite comparable with the poetry of this most singular genius; Villon had intensity and range, Donne added to it daring in form, Hopkins has the same intensity and yet a more daring form made to fit piercing passion, crucifixion in every word, and to convey, as in the case of Donne, the most complex emotion-laden thought. He testifies to the way in which a genius, unavoidably aware of the latent forces of his age, discovers truth through his own individual vision.[1]

Another preoccupation shared in varying degrees and aspects by all symbolists was music. The great revelation for their age was the music of Wagner, but there was more to it than that. Music offered them the perfect analogy for the fleetingness and elusiveness of their poetic experiences. Music meant above all a suggestive indefiniteness of vague emotive states favourable to the birth and, for the reader, the rebirth of the poetic experience. To take back from music what poets had lost to it was symbolism's avowed aim, yet amongst the most important poets no two conceptions were quite alike, and Mallarmé's conception was the most singular of all; he could never admit the predominance of music over the word, which alone could stand for *l'idée*. For Wagner, music is the crown of all the arts because it rises above the 'contingent' and moves in the sphere of essences. For Schelling, music is the archetypal rhythm of nature, it is a concept very similar to Plato's and Schopenhauer's and it stands for what is eternal in creation. For Baudelaire, music stood for the interchangeability of the arts and for fluidity; it was something similar for Verlaine; for Poe, it was above all indefiniteness. Wagner's opera was total art; it included décor, poetry, mime and music, and it was meant to express without distortion the whole experience of the artist; it was both mythical and musical, and its legendary foundations offered the widest appeal to human and also to racial feelings. The preoccupation with music and poetry was widespread in Germany, England and also in France, and was certainly anterior to Wagner and to Poe. Amongst those who have

[1] Hopkins has many points of resemblance with Mallarmé. Both poets, possessed by strong ideals, submit language to a most rigorous discipline in order that their ideal may be brought to life in poetry; in both cases the analogy with music is very strong, and Hopkins uses musical notations to indicate the quantity of a word; both believe that scanning is not a matter of individual lines, but that "a stanza is a long strain", as Hopkins says, and in the case of Mallarmé the scanning extends over the whole poem, if it is not a long one.

expressed the view that poetry is suggestive of music, few have
given a better explanation than Carlyle:

> Musical: how much lies in that! A musical thought is
> one spoken by a mind that has penetrated into the inmost
> heart of the thing; detected the inmost mystery of it,
> namely the *melody* that lies hidden in it; the inward har-
> mony of coherence which is its soul, whereby it exists,
> and has a right to be, here in this world. All inmost things,
> we may say, are melodious; naturally utter themselves in
> Song. The meaning of Song goes deep. Who is there that,
> in logical words, can express the effect music has on us?
> A kind of inarticulate unfathomable speech, which leads
> us to the edge of the Infinite, and lets us for moments gaze
> into that!
>
> . . . Observe too how all passionate language does of
> itself become musical,—with a finer music than the mere
> accent; the speech of a man even in zealous anger becomes
> a chant, a song. All deep things are Song. It seems some-
> how the very central essence of us, Song. . . .[1]

As far as similarities of views are concerned, it would be
difficult to find anything closer to the Mallarméan conception
of music, the very essence towards which poetry tends—the
absolute where Saint Cecilia stands, not with musical instruments and symphonies, but as 'musicienne du silence'.
Mallarmé had a clarity of vision unsurpassed in the literature
of his time, and a greater and greater tendency to pursue his
ideal—the absolute—with relentless consistency. The result
we shall see later; for the moment let us merely indicate in a
few words the necessary conclusions of symbolism.

Like every growth, it contains in itself the necessary developments which human terminology colours with æsthetic and
ethical connotations. At the purely biological level of cyclical
developments, decay and fall are nowhere nearer than at the

Heroes and Hero-worship (Collins), p. 110.

moment when the plant is in full blossom. Soon after that stage, leaves fall to earth to form compost food for new growth, and seeds fly in the wind towards other places and to rebirth. Ideas, like plants, grow to the point where they go to seed, decay and start again into new growth fertilised by new soil or new climates; it is part of the processes of nature. Kant and Hegel the greatest landmarks in philosophy since Plato, mark the point where the idealism of Plato and its various developments some positive, some negative, some lost in undergrowths through compressions or obstacles had harmonised themselves in a new healthy whole which reconciled the phenomenal world with the ideal, the apprehending subject with the universalism of mind. With Mallarmé, the phenomenal world disappears, negated by the subject"Moi projeté absolu." There is only the poet in the poetic act. The poetic act is language, therefore language is all; words are the only true reality, and if one breaks them as monkeys break coconuts, one might find inside the miraculous milk, unless in the course of awkward gestures one lets the whole thing fall to the ground, and then all is lost. Such was the end of Gertrude Stein and many others who followed in her wake and in that of James Joyce, But, of course, there is more to it than that in Joyce. The dream, the inner world beyond consciousness and the orderly apprehension of the senses was one of the main directions of symbolism groping for more complex, unexplored fields. But in the end, men forgot to return from these dark caves of the subconscious which they were quarrying for new jewels. They forgot the other world, the world of light, and they remained there in the dark shouting their enthusiasm or their joys, hoping that their inarticulate cries might be heard from above. Yet in vain, for they were beyond the human, and their exertions could only delight themselves; the few who returned tried to communicate the memories of their strange journey by pouring forth helter-skelter debris of words or images hastily snatched from the dark where they had been. This was surrealism. Reality, or society, was abject, vulgar, unbearable, therefore, let us go through it with a revolver, said André Breton, and so it was that we moved from the ivory tower of the symbolists towards the dark solipsistic cell and the final suicidal journeys of the surrealists.

The development which followed was normal, inescapable. Since there is nothing but the self which contains all this abhorred reality, we must destroy the self and its expression— language—by suicide or madness, said the surrealists. That marks the end of some aspects of a great idea, the end of branches which had followed the usual Heraclytean pattern of developping their opposites, but not the end of the main idea or stem which supports the whole. The symbolists, by concentrating on their private visions, severed themselves from life and pursued their æsthetic aims to the point where, as in *Axël's Castle* or in Huysmans's novel *A Rebours*, the hero wishes "to hide himself away from the world, in some street where he might deaden the sound of the loud rumbling of inflexible life".[1] Baudelaire did not care to hide himself; he was too proud for that, and he wore his dandyism, his boredom and his disgust for a society lost in the love of material amenities, as a mark of defiance. He felt that since he was so glaringly obvious in the eyes of the populace, he would make himself more obvious still, and singularise himself by cultivating his hysteria, in the same way as Rimbaud cultivated his 'dérègle-ment des sens' to the verge of madness. By the time of Mallarmé, the poet was so completely estranged from society that all hopes to convert, transform or shake that society had to be abandoned; it was best not to fight openly but to disguise oneself as a plain man engaged in the innocent occupation of schoolmastering—in reality meeting every now and then one's *Carbonari* friends and communicating to them messages which nobody else but themselves could understand, and which told of the absolute, and how to reach it. Mallarmé's apparent

[1] C. M. Bowra, op. cit., p. 13.

respectability is far more destructive and subversive than Baudelaire's or Rimbaud's rebellions; he does not rebel against reality, he destroys it and replaces it by the poetic act, which becomes transcendental and is only the means to reach the ideal; yet, in as far as it is an act, it has unbearable limitations in itself, self-contradicting the ideal the absolute which is its goal, so that the end is paralysis; as the poet's only reality is the poem and the poem in itself is an illusion, the poet remains a ghost in an uninhabitable world:

> Fantôme qu'à ce lieu son pur éclat assigne,
> Il s'immobilise au songe froid de mépris
> Que vêt parmi l'exil inutile le Cygne.[1]

The public answered contempt with contempt, and when, like Wilde, the artist tried to impose his views on a society which he had taunted the reaction was violent and with costly results to the writer. To be disconnected from life became for the æsthetes and would-be poets an end in itself, a means to reach the esoteric, byzantine temple which only the few initiated ones could enter; and later on these æsthetes passed from byzantinism to the open rebellion of the surrealists. The feeling of estrangement from society, and the desire not to speak directly in the first person continued to play a part in poetry and no doubt partly account for Yeats' theory of the mask and Ezra Pound's use of a 'persona'.

Mallarmé's example was not lost; Valéry realised the impossibility of equating poetry with the absolute and of reducing life to *le livre* or to an act of mind. He realised that life is meant to be lived and not to be annihilated in order to reach the absolute or to fill up *le néant*, 'le creux toujours futur'; together with him, the second wave of important symbolist poets like Yeats, Claudel, Eliot and Maeterlinck brings a reborn sensibility and a fresh approach to reality. The sense of mystery remains, music is still an important prerequisite of poetry, but

---

[1] Mallarmé, *Le vierge, le vivace et le bel aujourd'hui* . . .

the poet has reassumed his pristine rôle in society; he wishes to warn his fellow-beings and to testify to the existence of forces which might crush or save man, he is fully aware that the phenomenal world is the only way to approach the ideal and that eternity is reached through time. W. B. Yeats soon discarded the vague, dreamy quality of his early poetry to concentrate on life and on the realities of human emotions experienced at the individual and at the national level; human love, and the love of country conveyed through legends and myths hallowed by history, are the symbols, the objective correlatives which he uses in order to carry the weight of his emotions and thoughts. Eliot wrote *The Waste Land*, which is still the most profound and disturbing assessment of the ills of our age. They all took to drama, the most social of the arts, and T. S. Eliot and Claudel are undeniably among the greatest poet-dramatists of the last two hundred and fifty years. All of them, instead of standing aside from society or of merely screeching warnings of disasters, offered solutions to contemporary problems and pointed to certain directions where, according to them, lay salvation. All of them show in some of their best poetry, which embodies various aspects of the truth of our time and of all time, that the poet is neither an outcast or a misfit, nor a nightingale in the wilderness, but a man like the others, yet having in him so much more of the essence that he can more often than others connect with it and tell them what Truth might be and what is the meaning of its external signs or forms. Leaving out the self-conscious æsthetics and the didactic aspects of symbolism as a movement originally confined to France, the post-symbolist poets, whether these mentioned or those unmentioned yet, like Rilke, Stefan George or D'Annunzio, continue their predecessors in more than one respect. The use of symbols, allegories and legends to convey the poetic experience may be less self-conscious than with the preceding age; but poetry is still on the whole indirect or oblique and not direct; the poem, as Eliot said, is what it is and not what it says, and that after all is the main difference between conceptual poetry and poetry of discovery. Above all, the post-symbolist poets remain in some ways faithful to Mallarmé's view, which was also that of Flaubert, that the world could be saved by a better literature; yet literature, though a means to reach certain aspects of transcendence, is no longer transcendental in itself, but tends more and more to be the expression of man's wholly integrated personality, part of an integrated universe.

NOTE

The terms 'symbole', 'symbolique' and even 'symbolisme' were used in French literary history and criticism long before 1885. They were used by Alexandre Guiraud in 1824 in *La Muse Française*, by Jouffroy in 1843 in his *Cours d'Esthétique*, by Scudo in abuse of Wagner in the *Revue des Deux Mondes*, 1860 and 1861, and frequently by Baudelaire in both poetry and prose. But we have to wait until 1885 to find them used in order to define a school of poets.

The publication of Huysmans's *A Rebours* (1884) with its hero, Des Esseintes, and of *Les Déliquescences d'Adoré Floupette* (1885) roused violent criticism. In an article in *Le Temps*, 6 August 1885, Paul Bourde made great play with the words 'décadent' and 'décadisme'. That upset the young men who had gathered round Verlaine and Mallarmé, and who wanted a reply; Jean Moréas, the 'théoricien' of the group, undertook to give it, in *Le XIXe siècle*, 11 August 1885; there he laid down the principles of the new æsthetic, and rejected the label 'décadents' in the following words: "Les poètes décadents—la critique, puisque sa manie d'étiquetage est incurable, pourrait les appeler plus justement des *symbolistes*—que M. Bourde a estrapadés d'une main courtoise sont: MM. Stéphane Mallarmé, Paul Verlaine, Laurent Tailhade, Charles Vignier, Charles Morice et le signataire de cet article."[1]

[1] G. Michaud, *Message poétique du Symbolisme* (Nizet, Paris, 1947), vol. iv, p. 99.

Yet the term 'décadents' survived and was used defiantly by Anatole Baju, who, on 10 April 1886, founded *Le Décadent*. Some time later the editor of the *Figaro* thought of asking for an article on the main ideas of the new school, and once more Jean Moréas wrote a manifesto, published in the *Figaro Littéraire*, 18 September 1886. These are some extracts from that text, supplied by Michaud:

> Depuis deux ans, la presse parisienne s'est beaucoup occupée d'une école de poètes et de prosateurs dits *décadents*. Le conteur du *Thé chez Miranda* (en collaboration avec M. Paul Adam, l'auteur de *Soi*), le poète des *Syrtes* et des *Cantilènes*, M. Jean Moréas, un des plus en vue parmi ces révolutionnaires des lettres, a formulé, sur notre demande, pour les lecteurs du *Supplément*, les principes fondamentaux de la nouvelle manifestation d'art (p. 23) (Editor of the *Figaro*).
>
> Nous avons déjà proposé la dénomination de SYMBOLISME comme la seule capable de désigner raisonnablement la tendance actuelle de l'esprit créateur en art. Cette dénomination peut être maintenue (p. 24) (Moréas).

After this, and the publication of the short-lived periodical *Le Symboliste* by Moréas, Kahn and Adam in 1886, the new name was established, though echoes of 'décadent' could still be heard faintly. Anatole Baju's words are worth quoting in this respect: "Par respect pour le maître qui a formulé le premier la doctrine symbolique, Stéphane Mallarmé, il ne m'est pas permis de combattre le symbolisme. Je l'admets en poésie mais pas ailleurs."[1] Together with this text one should quote also the following: "Nous ne considérons le terme symbolisme que comme une étiquette désignant les poètes idéalistes de notre génération. C'est une épithète commode et rien de plus."[2]

[1] *Le Décadent*, 1886.
[2] Adolphe Retté in *La Plume*, 15 February 1892.

The most important poets connected with the symbolist movement were Baudelaire, then Verlaine, Mallarmé and Rimbaud, each one with certain definite leanings, Verlaine towards affectivity, Mallarmé towards intellect, Rimbaud towards fantasy. With Verlaine one generally connects those who are described as the decadents: Laforgue, Corbière, Samain, Le Cardonnel, Guérin and, in some distant ways, Proust. With Mallarmé one connects first and foremost Valéry, then, together with him, a group of poets who seem to have as much in common with Verlaine and the decadents as with Mallarmé: they are Moréas, Ghil, Maeterlinck, Stuart Merrill, Dujardin, Fontainas, Mockel, Francis Jammes, Viélé-Griffin, Paul Fort, and Verhaeren, who is not without affinities with Claudel. With Rimbaud one connects St. Pol Roux, Apollinaire, the surrealists and Claudel, but a Claudel who, naturally, has nothing to do with surrealism, who believes that creation is God's poem or God's word, and that the poet's task is to find the true metaphor and, by naming, to replace everything in the divine order which is movement, the sense of which is partly revealed by man's action. Mallarmé and Valéry dreamt of 'la poésie pure', the surrealists of 'la vie pure', Claudel of revealing the essence and thereby of co-operating with God in the creation of the world.

CHAPTER III

The influence of Poe on Mallarmé according to the critics

IN an essay first published in 1920 (later collected in *Variété II*: 'Situation de Baudelaire'), Valéry, who already had some of his greatest achievements behind him, sums up his two great predecessors' opinions about Poe, in terms as enthusiastic as they are precise, and leaves no doubt as to the debt that, according to him, French poetry owed to Poe. Valéry was not given to enthusiasm, he was a worshipper of calm, empyrean detachment, and although he was, like everybody else, liable to errors of judgment, the careful wording of his views, in a writer who, like him, always wrote at the extreme point of consciousness, makes clear the genuineness and, as far as he was concerned, the rationality of his admiration for Poe. This is what he says:

> Baudelaire . . . était né sensuel et précis; il était d'une sensibilité dont l'exigence le conduisait aux recherches les plus délicates de la forme; mais ces dons n'eussent fait de lui qu'un émule de Gautier, sans doute, ou un excellent artiste du Parnasse, s'il n'eût, par la curiosité de son esprit, mérité la chance de découvrir dans les ouvrages d'Edgar Poe un nouveau monde intellectuel. Le démon de la lucidité, le génie de l'analyse, et l'inventeur des combinaisons les plus neuves et les plus séduisantes de la logique avec l'imagination, de la mysticité avec le calcul, le psychologue de l'exception, l'ingénieur littéraire qui approfondit et utilise toutes les ressources de l'art, lui apparaissent en Edgar Poe

et l'émerveillent. Tant de vues originales et de promesses extraordinaires l'ensorcellent. Son talent en est transformé, sa destinée en est magnifiquement changée.[1]

How could any reader's mind avoid the dazzling effect of such coruscating epithets or the pervading power of the eulogistic tone? The attempt could no doubt be made, but this is not the place for it; let us, on the contrary, see if the reader could accept still more and acquiesce and admire.

> Jamais [continues Valéry] le problème de la littérature n'avait été jusqu'à Edgar Poe examiné dans ses prémisses, réduit à un problème de psychologie, abordé au moyen d'une analyse où la logique et la mécanique des effets était délibérément employées.[2]

And further:

> Toute son œuvre manifeste à chaque page l'acte d'une intelligence et d'une volonté qui ne s'observent, à ce degré, dans aucune autre carrière littéraire.[3]

But let us move now, from the plane of generalities, to a few concrete examples as brought forth by Valéry in the same essay:

> Poe a compris que la poésie moderne devait se conformer à la tendance d'une époque qui a vu se séparer de plus en plus nettement les modes et les domaines de l'activité et qu'elle pouvait prétendre à réaliser son projet propre et à se produire en quelque sorte, à l'état pur. . . . Ainsi, analyse de la volupté poétique, définition par exhaustion de la poésie absolue,—Poe montrait une voie, il enseignait une doctrine très séduisante et très rigoureuse dans laquelle une sorte de mathématique et une sorte de mystique s'unissaient. . . .[4]

[1] *Variété II* (édition de la N.R.F., 1927), vol. vii, p. 147.
[2] Ibid., p. 156.   [3] Ibid., p. 157.
[4] Ibid., p. 160.

Here we have the key words mentioned: *purity* and mathematical *perfection*. The theory of Art for Art's sake and the perfection of form of the Parnassians are transposed into Poe's æsthetic and seem to emerge from that transposition with specifically Poesque colours. Yet that theory was already well established in France without the slightest need of Poe's influence. Is it because "il n'y a pas de grand homme pour son valet", or because "on va chercher bien loin ce que l'on a sous la main", or is it because of a strange revulsion which ever leads us to the rejection of our father's virtues and to the admiration of those same virtues in anyone who is beyond our affective field? The fact is that Gautier, Heredia, Banville and other masters all melted away in the glow of Poe's sun, and that he alone remained to be gazed at with reverence by three generations of French poets. And Valéry continues:

> L'œuvre de Baudelaire est remarquablement conforme aux préceptes de Poe. Les *Fleurs du Mal* ne contiennent ni poèmes historiques ni légendes; rien qui repose sur un récit, on n'y voit point de tirades philosophiques. La politique n'y paraît, les descriptions y sont rares et toujours significatives. Mais tout y est charme, musique, sensualité puissante et abstraite. . . . Luxe, forme et volupté.[1]

In brief, we have here the careful avoidance of all the romantic defects, something of which Baudelaire was already very conscious before he read Poe; for he knew that, if he was going to be a poet, he had to be Baudelaire and not Victor Hugo. At the same time, this definition of Baudelaire's poetry applies exactly to that of Valéry, and of course to Mallarmé's about whom Valéry says:

> Quant à Stéphane Mallarmé, dont les premiers vers pourraient se confondre aux plus beaux vers et aux plus denses des *Fleurs du Mal*, il a poursuivi dans leurs conséquences les plus subtiles les recherches formelles et

[1] *Variété II*, vol. vii, p. 161.

techniques dont les analyses d'Edgar Poe et les essais et les commentaires de Baudelaire lui avaient communiqué la passion et enseigné l'importance. Tandis que Verlaine et Rimbaud ont continué Baudelaire dans l'ordre du sentiment et de la sensation, Mallarmé l'a prolongé dans le domaine de la perfection et de la pureté poétique.[1]

We should not leave Valéry without examining one of his most important texts about the problem of influence and about his views on Mallarmé—his *Lettre-Préface* to Royère's study of Mallarmé. There we not only find an enumeration of the qualities which Valéry most admired in Mallarmé's poetry, but also a confession which his analytical mind and his honesty could not fail to make and which is, that in describing Mallarmé's work he does what, in one way or another, all critics do, he describes his own work, his own ambitions and his own admirations: "Voilà ce que je prêtais à Mallarmé: un ascétisme trop conforme, peut-être, à mes jugements sur les Lettres, que j'ai toujours regardées avec de grands doutes sur leur vraie valeur."[2]

We shall see later how, in a similar way, Mallarmé, talking about Poe, also talks about himself. For the moment let us remember one other important aspect which limits considerably Poe's influence on Mallarmé, namely the reference made by Valéry to Villiers de l'Isle-Adam and his influence on Mallarmé:

> Son esprit, pour solitaire et autonome qu'il se fût fait, avait reçu quelque impression des prestigieuses et fantastiques improvisations de Villiers de l'Isle-Adam, et jamais ne s'était tout à fait détaché d'une certaine métaphysique.
> . . . C'est ainsi qu'il en est venu à vouloir donner à l'art d'écrire un sens universel, *une valeur d'univers*; et qu'il a reconnu que le suprême objet du monde, et la justification

[1] *Variété II*, vol. vii, p. 165.
[2] Royère, op. cit., pp. 24–5.

de son existence,—(pour autant que l'on accordât cette existence)—était, ne pouvait être qu'un *Livre*.[1]

This is the very core of Mallarmé's æsthetics.

Mallarmé, says Lemonnier,[2] read Poe in English and wanted to continue Baudelaire's task of presenting his poetry to the French. He too, like Baudelaire, Lemonnier continues,[3] praises Poe for having tried to produce each time a unique masterpiece. Poe's style, according to Mallarmé, is "ou fulgurant ou translucide, pur comme le diamant", and for both of them poetry and music were forms of art which are extremely close; but Lemonnier remarks that: "Poe ne paraît avoir goûté que la musique des mots, alors que chez Mallarmé le culte profond de toute musique rejoignait cette aspiration vers la certitude et la béatitude idéale qui pour les deux hommes est le but même de la poésie."[4] According to him Mallarmé has strained the analogy between Poe and himself when he praises Poe for having tried to give "un sens plus pur aux mots de la tribu". His view is that Mallarmé resembles Poe in as far as Poe was different from Baudelaire. He points out the fact that, while the latter was at war with society, the two former endeavoured to accept it, Mallarmé with success, Poe through repeated defeats; and he notes that Baudelaire was sensuous while Poe and Mallarmé, in spite of his preoccupations with sex, were rather chaste, living on frozen heights, without being either haunted or horrified by original sin, yet passionately attached to pure ideas and concerned, even more than Baudelaire, with perfection of form. Poe has, according to Lemonnier, a sense of drama completely lacking in Mallarmé; if both can be said to be intellectuals in love with systems and ideas, Poe believes in science and positivism, Mallarmé is on the contrary a metaphysician. In order to reach the ecstasy of

[1] Royère, op. cit., p. 13.
[2] 'Edgar Poe et les poètes français' (*Nouvelle Revue Critique*, Paris, 1932), p. 13.
[3] Ibid., p. 93.   [4] Ibid.

absolute certitude, Poe relies on beauty, Mallarmé on more complex means.[1]

Lemonnier points out that Mallarmé stated that "he learnt English only to read Poe", and that "therefore Poe enabled Mallarmé to find the means of his livelihood":[2] "Il est possible", he says, "que l'influence de Poe se soit exercée plus sur la vie de Mallarmé que sur son œuvre; car les traces précises que l'on en trouve dans ses poèmes ne sont point nombreuses et elles sont toutes superficielles";[3] and he suggests that "Mallarmé may have remembered Poe's poem *To Zante*, when he wrote:

> Une ruine, par mille écumes bénie,
> Sous l'hyacinthe, au loin, de ses jours triomphaux."[4]

He notes that *La Prose pour Des Esseintes* is pervaded with a Poesque atmosphere, and that Huysmans's hero, as is well known, is a great admirer of Poe. He thinks that Des Esseintes is, in Mallarmé's mind, closely associated with Roderick Usher, and he sees in the poem itself definite traces of Poe's influence, but goes on to suggest that there is another poem which bears even more traces of Poe's influence, the sonnet which begins:

> Sur le bois oublié quand passe l'hiver sombre . . .[5]

This, according to him, is a poem in which Mallarmé is more Poesque than Poe himself. True enough, the reminiscences of *The Raven*—midnight, the setting, the atmosphere, "le souffle de mon nom murmuré tout un soir"—are undeniable.

Lemonnier concludes by saying that Mallarmé has really applied these theories of pure poetry which Poe had merely advocated without putting them into practice. According to him, the influence on Mallarmé of Stuart Merrill's idealism,

---

[1] Lemonnier, op. cit., p. 96.
[2] Ibid., p. 97. [3] Ibid., p. 98. [4] Ibid.
[5] Mallarmé, *Œuvres Complètes* (Gallimard, Paris, 1945), p. 69.

that of Carlyle, and above all that of Hegel, are far more important than that of Poe. To these influences he adds the possible influence of St. Martin, in whose work one can find the whole of Mallarmé's doctrine on the dignity of speech, and also the best definition of symbolism:

> St. Martin aimait à poursuivre à chaque instant, sous tous ses voiles, l'éternelle métaphore de la nature visible, traduction incomplète et altérée de l'invisible nature et de l'éternel univers. . . . St. Martin avait un respect religieux, un culte pour la parole, expression et symbole du Verbe éternel. Venue de Dieu, elle doit retourner à Dieu. Elle habite parmi les merveilles divines; c'est là son centre et comme sa patrie naturelle.[1]

These ideas are also those of Mallarmé, and Lemonnier concludes:

> Que nous sommes loin ici de Poe et de son système superficiel et purement psychologique! Si Poe a agi sur Mallarmé ce fut au début de sa vie comme un simple excitant. L'œuvre de Poe fut le tremplin truqué d'où Mallarmé s'élança vers l'infini. . . . Pour les maîtres du symbolisme Poe fut entièrement mais uniquement un initiateur.[2]

Then further: "Poe has given symbolist poets their general concept of poetry; like him they have wanted it to be a music, like him they have wanted it to suggest a superior reality, and they have tried to keep alive his sense of mystery. But he did not supply them with the necessary materials—symbols and free verse—which enabled them to raise the edifice whose main outline he only suggested. He brought to these poets a group of new images and feelings which contributed to the growth of *l'esprit de décadence*. . . . If that *esprit de décadence*

[1] Quoted by Lemonnier, op. cit., p. 105, as being an extract from a book published in 1852 by Caro on St. Martin.
[2] Op cit., pp. 105–6.

went very soon out of fashion, the concept of pure poetry still seems to be the only one possible."[1] Professor Mansell Jones says:

> . . . the cult of perfection in its modern phase belongs to the Gautier-Baudelaire-Flaubert tradition,[2] coming to its most exigent consciousness in Mallarmé, 'martyr de l'idée du parfait', as his disciple Valéry called him. In origin it is a plastic-Parnassian conception; it has nothing to do with E. A. Poe. His French admirers, however, obsessed with their traditional ideal and unconsciously fusing it with the notion of purity, developed with many elaborations and subtleties from the simple formulae of *The Poetic Principle*, have persistently read it back into Poe's work.[3]

A critic whose work on Mallarmé cannot be overlooked is Noulet. Her aims were different from those of Thibaudet in *La Poésie de Mallarmé*,[4] which remains the most penetrating and the most valid study of the poetry of this poet. Thibaudet did not have the evidence required in order to relate the life of the poet to his work, says Charles Mauron.[5] I should be more inclined to say that he did not want it and he did not need it. His aim was to appraise and to assess as well as he could through his subjective sensitiveness and in the light of his historical knowledge of poetry, the poetry of Mallarmé. That he does, in a way which leaves behind as merely interesting sidelights all the attempts by Charles Mauron, Mary

---

[1] Op. cit., pp. 199–200.

[2] Charles Chassé, in *Les Clefs de Mallarmé* (Aubier, Paris, 1954), p. 16, says: Les hommes du Second Empire, très réalistes, avaient été profondément influencés par les théories rigides d'Auguste Comte . . . les poètes étaient des Parnassiens pour qui le monde extérieur seul existait et qui, comme Verlaine à ses débuts, se bornaient à "ciseler des vers comme des coupes". Throughout the whole second half of the nineteenth century, Flaubert, among others, never ceased to warn against inspiration and to advocate impersonality, objectivity and the cult of beauty—an ideal more Greek than Christian.

[3] *The Background of Modern French Poetry* (C.U.P., 1951), p. 56.

[4] Edition de la N.R.F., Paris, 1913.

[5] *Mallarmé l'Obscur* (édition Denoël, Paris, 1941), p. 6.

Bonaparte or Gaston Bachelard to relate Mallarmé's life to his poetry. I share Albert Béguin's views as stated in his introduction to *L'Ame Romantique et le Rêve*, where he says that: "il veut étudier les œuvres poétiques en tant qu'œuvres constituées, mais qu'il n'a que faire des savants—les psychanalystes—qui prétendent en trouver les ressorts psychiques." No amount of psychoanalytical research into the mother-complex of Baudelaire or of Rimbaud will add anything whatever to our appreciation or enjoyment of their poetry. Noulet's study of Mallarmé is not an attempt to delve into the poet's complexes and repressions with the hope of returning to the surface with the pearl which is the poetry. She does relate the poetic creation to the life of the poet, but she does so purely to show us the growth and various aspects of Mallarmé's poetic genius. Her method of investigation is orthodox without being ossified, penetrating without being too one-sided. Operating, as she does, from the safe ground of scholarly research, she has plenty to say about influences and affiliations, and naturally she deals extensively with those related to Poe: "The reading of Poe's works inclined Mallarmé towards doctrines of literary composition which by nature he was predisposed to accept. To translate Poe meant for him to reflect about a method of willed creation which he adopts and adapts according to his gifts; it also meant the growth of linguistic habits, partly conscious, partly accidental, which aimed at bringing together and attempting to fuse, sometimes without success, the geniuses of the English and the French language."[1] This seems to me a very interesting remark, well grounded on facts. I am not so happy with the parallelism between *The Raven* and *L'Azur* which follows; I do not find it convincing; *L'Azur* seems to me dramatic as most poetry is, because it is a resolution of conflicts, but it is not a dramatic story in verse in the same way as *The Raven* is. Mallarmé's poem is not a narrative, though it

[1] Noulet, *L'œuvre poétique de Stéphane Mallarmé* (Droz, Paris, 1940), p. 152.

has a coherence which unfolds along well-known lines of rhetoric: statement of theme, various possibilities, and resolution—or rather conclusion. Every expression of human emotion, even in madness, has some kind of logic, whether it is rational logic or affective logic, and every poem must have a definite congruence to the central theme. Mallarmé was, like so many of his contemporaries, a very self-conscious artist; that self-consciousness, although it is exhibited in Poe's theories, yet not much in his poetry, was part of a generalised attitude which goes far beyond Poe, an attitude which is partly a reaction against the glorified egotism of the romantic age, and partly a greater and greater awareness of the way a work of art comes to life, an attitude which, in the end, will resolve itself in the concentration of interest on language for language's sake. Noulet has no serious doubts about the genuineness of *The Philosophy of Composition*, or about its influence on Mallarmé, who, according to her, tried to put these theories into practice: "Il essaie de mettre en pratique la méthode de Poe; elle dirigea ses travaux, elle conduisit son analyse mentale jusqu'aux finalités extrêmes."[1]

The reverence which Mallarmé had for Poe is beyond question. Noulet rightly points out that although Mallarmé admired Baudelaire, he never calls him 'grand Maître'—that is a title reserved to Poe alone, whose influence, according to Noulet,[2] was more lasting.

> D'où lui est venue l'idée d'user de la répétition de si nouvelle et captieuse façon? Imite-t-il? Innove-t-il? Il suit un conseil. Le poète qu'il admire entre tous, Edgar Poe, avait écrit dans une page célébrée par Baudelaire que le refrain était "de tous les effets d'art connus, celui qui était le plus généralement employé".[3]

Commenting on *L'Azur*, Noulet writes:

[1] Noulet: *L'œuvre poétique de Stéphane Mallarmé* (Droz, Paris, 1940), p. 158.
[2] Ibid., p. 150.   [3] Ibid., p. 110.

L'idée de la quadruple répétition à l'intérieur d'un même vers a peut-être été inspirée au poète par Edgar Poe dont il était en train de traduire *Les Cloches*.[1]

On that specific problem, even M. Scherer concedes that Mallarmé may have been influenced by Poe through Baudelaire.[2]

When it comes to the problem of translation, Noulet has some very interesting things to say. Her analysis of the feelings which are part of the incomplete knowledge of a language is both acute and pertinent to the case of Mallarmé. English being the source of his livelihood, he certainly had a profound though erratic knowledge of it as a language, and also of its literature. He could not claim to be bilingual,[3] as Du Bos for instance nearly was, but the slight errors which we find in his translation do not by any means disqualify him as a translator. There are many who know less of a language than Mallarmé knew of English, and yet, they are better translators than he is. But there are not a few who know, or are supposed to know, more English than Mallarmé knew, and who can easily accumulate a greater ratio of errors per page than he ever did. I know that Viélé-Griffin has listed the various mistakes which Mallarmé made in his translation. I agree that Mallarmé could not grasp the full meaning of certain off-the-ground expressions, and even less the affective climate and subtle connotations of certain words. He did not, he could not know the soul of the English language, therefore he could not live through it. But he could attempt to translate from it, with the same

[1] Noulet, *L'œuvre poétique de Stéphane Mallarmé* (Droz, Paris, 1940), p. 71.
[2] J. Sherer, *L'Expression littéraire dans l'œuvre de Mallarmé* (Droz, Paris, 1947), p. 218.
[3] A. Schweitzer says on the matter of bilingualism in *My Life and Thought*, translated by C. T. Campion (Allen and Unwin, 1933), p. 78:
"My own experience makes me think it only self-deception if any believes that he has two mother-tongues. He may think that he is equally master of each, yet it is invariably the case that he actually thinks only in one, and is only in that one really free and creative."

possibilities of success as any poet who ever attempted to turn the poetry of another language into his own. Poe was not Homer or Aeschylus; his words neither depict accurately nor burn with the fire of passion; they convey an atmosphere, they are part of an orchestration. Mallarmé had a very difficult task, technically a more difficult task than that of Chapman or Shelley, infinitely more difficult than that of Gide turning the Rembrandt-like complexity of *Hamlet* into a Courbet-like simplicity and accuracy of lines as Gide saw them. Who has ever translated poetry, indirect poetry, satisfactorily for both the purists and the lovers of poetry? There is an undisguised strain of the pedant's tone in Viélé-Griffin counting the solecisms and inaccuracies of 'l'élève Mallarmé', and in M. Scherer opining to his magisterial verdict.

Mallarmé was a poet whose imagination could cast wrong colours on the words he was trying to translate. True enough, "with many a flirt and flutter" is not "avec maints enjouement et agitation d'ailes", and 'presently' is not 'subitement' but 'bientôt'. But I infinitely prefer as being more poetically true, yet less pedestrianly exact, Mallarmé's rendering of "Whose fiery eyes now burned into my bosom's/Core" to that of Viélé-Griffin.[1] "Dévoré par la lumière de la lampe" has more poetic vitality than the "où la lumière de la lampe épandait un regard avide" suggested by Viélé-Griffin for a translation of "which the lamp gloated o'er". One may or may not appreciate the flavour of the very Mallarméan translation of "and the silken, sad, uncertain rustling", but one would have been much happier if Viélé-Griffin had been able to point out what he thought was faulty and suggest an alternative. There is the word 'purpural': it is indeed a word which dates, but that is about all one can say about it. But as for the damning of 'quiétude' as being a *contre-sens* for 'darkness', this is surely putting strong strains on terminology. The relation between the two terms is surely sufficiently close—one being the normal

[1] Given in Mallarmé's *Œuvres Complètes*, p. 1524.

psychic concomitant of the other—to render their interpolarity in poetry more than grammatically acceptable. For Mallarmé, phenomenon and apprehension, matter and spirit are never separated; he always brings together sensation and its intellectual meaning, a picture and the feelings attached to it; but what is most important to him is the meaning and the affective connotations of the picture. Juxtaposition and transposition are for him normal processes; so we have "nuit hagarde", "sanglotante idée", and "et de la soie l'incertain et triste bruissement".

All this reminds one of La Fontaine's *Les Animaux Malades de la Peste*—whatever the poor donkey does tips the scales against him; and yet, here as well as there, though the donkey be eaten by his fellow-animals, and Mallarmé be capped with the donkey's ears, "il n'y a pas là de quoi faire fouetter un chat". How apposite are a poet's views—Rossetti's—on the translation of poetry: "The life-blood of rhythmical translation is this commandment: that a good poem shall not be turned into a bad one. The only motive of putting poetry into a fresh language must be to endow a fresh nation, if possible, with one more possession of beauty. Poetry not being an exact science, literality of rendering is altogether secondary to this chief law, yet when it can be obtained, the translation is fortunate to unite them." [1]

Mallarmé was not a philologist, and he does not deserve the carping remarks which are prompted by M. Scherer's laboratory purism. It is true that Mallarmé has got the wrong shade and above all the wrong grammatical connection of the word 'enchanted'; it is true that he uses neologisms such as 'pallide' and 'scoriaque'—a crime for a philologist—and that he prefers to translate 'pacified' by 'pacifier' instead of the more natural (*sic*) 'apaiser', but none of these so-called flaws affects the value of the translations; they may be picked out through a microscopic lens, but in the end they only belong to the laboratory

[1] D. G. Rossetti, *Early Italian Poets* (Oxford edition), pp. 175–6.

—after all, the English 'scoriac' is practically as odd as Mallarmé's neologism. As for the few hairs which M. Scherer splits over the translation of *The Conquering Worm* and *The Sleeper*, this seems to me using a sledge-hammer to squash a fly; if he cannot accept and appreciate the ambiguity of *pour le monde*, as being more apt in its context than the pedestrian and 'natural' *pour rien au monde*, then I fear he will always feel unhappy in the 'unnaturalness' of poetry. I do not need to comment on the remarks with which he concludes his appreciation of Mallarmé: "un amateur distingué parfois, et parfois hésitant". I am unfailingly reminded of the Lycée and the Bulletin Trimestriel; Mallarmé the pupil, and even, perhaps, the teacher, might have been described in these terms, but they ill apply to the poet translator of Poe; the confusion between the two is something worse than pedantism and unrepentant classroom manners.

One has the feeling that M. Scherer not only has a thesis with regard to Mallarmé's language, but also that he has the desire to remain faithful to a tradition of French grammarians who make comparisons with other languages almost invariably pan out in favour of French. He quotes his master Léon Lemonnier as saying that "l'anglais a nécessairement une syntaxe sans souplesse et sans subtilité",[1] then he partly contradicts and partly seeks to elaborate this statement in a way completely unsupported by evidence. He says: "La syntaxe anglaise déconcerte un esprit latin par son vague, son absence de règles strictes."[2] Then what is it, one may ask, that makes "la syntaxe anglaise sans souplesse", if there are no strict rules? The fact is that English syntax is more fluid, more subtle, more malleable than French, for it has been less tampered with by grammarians. And when M. Scherer makes the statement that in English "chaque mot peut y remplir n'importe quelle fonction",[3] he really makes one wonder that he should have dared to describe

[1] Sherer, op. cit., p. 30.
[2] Ibid.
[3] Ibid.

76

Mallarmé as an amateur. The English word is more autono-
mous than the French, it is more independent of grammar and
rhetoric, but it is a word and not a neutral sign. Mr. Gardner
Davies was very moderate when, in his review of M.Scherer's
book, he remarked that "M.Scherer somewhat arbitrarily sets
aside the influence of English on Mallarmé's syntax",[1] and he
left nobody in doubt about his views, which were very remote
from those of M. Scherer

How much more refreshing to come back to the balanced
views of Mme Noulet. First she quotes various critics, Roden-
bach, André Suarès, André Thérive,[2] all tending to show that
English poetry and English syntax had a profound influence on
Mallarmé; Thérive goes so far as to describe Mallarmé's style
as 'un style traduction'. To these critics one could add others
such as John Charpentier who, in his book *L'Evolution de la
Poésie Lyrique*,[3] states that Mallarmé was very much influenced
by English poetry and syntax; Mauclair stresses the same point,
and in his book *Princes de l'Esprit*[4] he talks of "une continuelle
souplesse de syntaxe très proche chez lui de la syntaxe anglaise".
The last to be quoted before returning to Noulet is Charles
Maurras, who, in an article in the *Figaro* following Mallarmé's
election as Prince of Poets, 27 January 1896, quotes with
approval the words of Louis Baragnon:

> Je suppose un aimable homme dont les habitudes vrai-
> ment maladives d'ironie laissaient intacte la fine érudition
> et l'aimable courtoisie, qui, nourri de Hoffman et de Poe,
> pense en allemand, construit en anglais et par une plaisan-
> terie suprême nous fasse l'honneur d'emprunter notre
> vocabulaire.

This kind of statement needs no comment, it is not meant to
draw any, it is only meant to amuse.

[1] *French Studies* (Basil Blackwell, Oxford, 1948), p. 181.
[2] Noulet, op. cit., p. 158.
[3] Editions des Œuvres Représentatives (Paris, 1930), pp. 202–3.
[4] Michel (Paris, 1931), p. 115.

Noulet's observations on Mallarmé's translations are skilful, sympathetic, and, on the whole, carry conviction. In conclusion this is what she says: "When one examines the influence of Mallarmé's translations on his style, it seems possible to say that the charm of translation has exercised a strong attraction on him. He saw in it a means of producing a poetical atmosphere together with a sense of mystery which differentiates poetry from every-day speech. He tried without ignoring the genius of his native language to imitate the supple and harmonious grace of English syntax." Then the argument continues along lines which could be summarised as follows. Was Mallarmé's style affected by a too prolonged contact with English? The examination of his translations does not permit a positive answer. That his readings and translations from English may have encouraged his leanings towards disobedience is a possibility. But the kind of submission which leads a language to fear any new form or any daring construction is not helpful to it. It is not at all certain that the exclusive use of one's native language favours its vitality and growth. It can easily lead to a jejune purism and a monotonous stiffness. Very often a literary language can only acquire vitality and growth through contact with a foreign language. The singularities, the idiosyncrasies and peculiarities which one may discover through a literal translation of a foreign language are very effective in bringing to light the flaws and nuances of one's native language. Was Ronsard not right to praise grafting, for why should that operation be less profitable in linguistics than in horticulture?[1] In the case of Mallarmé it is quite possible that a sufficient, yet incomplete knowledge of English, together with the exercise of translation, may have given to the French language an elasticity hitherto unexplored, a freedom in the

[1] I fully agree with these remarks of Noulet. Poets are the guardians of language, but they can only guard it by developing it, by increasing its vitality. Rationally applied semantic and syntactical transfusions from one form of speech or one language to another sharpen the resistance and increase the vitality of the recipient.

use of words hitherto unknown and a syntactic suppleness hitherto unwanted. But all those tendencies were present in Mallarmé's French before he began translating Poe.[1]

Charles Mauron, in his preface to his work on *Mallarmé l'Obscur*, says:

> Le Docteur Mondor croit que l'influence de Poe sur Mallarmé était plus profonde et plus durable que celle de Baudelaire. Ne faudrait-il pas plutôt parler de ressemblance? Car si Baudelaire agit d'abord sur la langue, le style, le sens de la beauté chez Mallarmé, il ne pouvait guère en être de même pour Poe en dépit des apparences.[2]

Mondor is convinced that "Mallarmé a remplacé, depuis quelques années, par celui d'Edgar Poe, le culte majeur qu'il avait pour Baudelaire",[3] and later on in his book he says: "Un homme, par sa pénétration, sa profondeur d'analyse, les ressources, l'étrangeté de son art, les calculs et l'extraordinaire sonorité de sa musique l'a conquis, c'est Edgar Poe."[4] According to Mondor,[5] Mallarmé, who was in the habit of reciting to himself "comme une prière, une phrase de Baudelaire sur leur maître commun",[6] set himself the task of removing "l'interdit

---

[1] The influence of Latin could account for some of his syntactic oddities as it accounts for some of Milton's, and for his stress on the importance of the phrase or the paragraph in contradistinction to the line. At the same period, and certainly on his own, G. M. Hopkins was insisting on the fact that a stanza was one long strain to be scanned as a unit and not line by line.

[2] Op. cit., p. xii.

[3] Mondor, *Vie de Mallarmé* (Gallimard, Paris, 1941), p. 197.

[4] Ibid., p. 325.

[5] Ibid., p. 41.

[6] The phrase is:

"Il lui sera donné de conquérir l'admiration des gens qui pensent par son amour du Beau, par sa connaissance des conditions harmoniques de la beauté, par la poésie profonde et plaintive ouvragée néanmoins, transparente et correcte comme un bijou de cristal, par son admirable style, pur et bizarre— serré comme les mailles d'une armure,—complaisant et minutieux,—et dont la plus légère intention sert à pousser doucement le lecteur vers un but voulu . . ."

(From Baudelaire, *Edgar Poe, sa vie et ses œuvres*, préface de la traduction des *Histoires Extraordinaires*.)

porté par Baudelaire", which was to the effect that Poe's poems could not be translated.

> L'influence de Poe s'est exercée sur son esprit depuis sa vingtième année. Il lui doit d'avoir élevé sa pensée et élargi sa sensibilité au-delà des limites du monde apparent. . . . Un jour, cette influence s'est même exercée sur la signature de Mallarmé. Il a emprunté, à partir de 1873, à son maître américain, un fragment de son paraphe.[1]

Charles Mauron disagrees with Mondor on that point of Poe's influence on Mallarmé, and he concludes by saying: "Mais je ne pense pas que, sans Poe, la production de Mallarmé eût été bien différente."[2]

Such seems to be, all in all, the predominant opinion. Thibaudet, in his searching study on the poetry of Mallarmé, hardly mentions Poe; he sees reminiscences of Poe in *Apparition* and *Fenêtres*, and talking about the sonnet *Le vierge, le vivace*, he suggests that: "Le motif initial en est peut-être une harmonie en blanc majeur suggérée par quelque spectacle d'hiver. Peut-être aussi Mallarmé a-t-il songé à une transposition en blanc du *Corbeau* qu'il traduisit."[3] But that is all he has to say about Poe's possible influence on Mallarmé.

Recently, in a brief essay called 'Poursuite de l'Ombre', published in *La Table Ronde*,[4] M. Michel Carrouges raised the problem of *The Raven*'s influence on *Igitur*. He finds, to begin with, striking resemblances between the two poems: the setting—in each case midnight—the bust of Pallas in Poe and the bust of a superior genius in Mallarmé, the same ominous curtains, the same bird with wings flapping in the dark night, and the same end—Poe's soul lies half-dead in the shade of the Raven, Igitur lays himself down on his ancestor's ashes; even the "Never more" of *The Raven* is echoed by the "Pas encore" of *Igitur*. But M. Carrouges wisely realises that the evidence

---

[1] Mondor, op. cit., p. 544.   [2] Op. cit., p. xiv.
[3] Op. cit., p. 169.   [4] August–September 1950.

remains very slim, that above all similar situations could easily produce similar reactions, and that what counts is not the influence of a poet on another, but the common archetypal source of their poetic experience, and the relation between the psyche of the two poets and their poetic experience. M. Carrouges dismisses Poe's theory on the composition of *The Raven* and starts from the premise that the poem expresses the most deep-set traits of Poe's personality. He quotes from Lauvrière's book, *Le génie morbide d'Edgar Poe* (p. 112), Poe's reply to a certain Cornelius Mathews, who was writing something on witchcraft and was discussing the problem with Poe, who, one day, said to him: "Why should you not have a bird of bad omen, a raven, flying over the sorcerer's head? This dæmonic bird haunts me, I cannot get rid of him; even here, I can hear him croaking as I could hear him at Stoke Newington; the beat of his wings is in my ears." Then side by side with this quotation M. Carrouges quotes Mallarmé's letter to Cazalis:

> Mais combien plus je l'étais [incapable de me distraire] il y a plusieurs mois, d'abord dans ma lutte avec ce vieux et méchant plumage, terrassé, heureusement, Dieu! Mais comme cette lutte s'était passée sur son aile osseuse, qui, par une agonie plus vigoureuse que je l'eusse soupçonnée chez lui, m'avait emporté dans des ténèbres, je tombai victorieux—éperdument et infiniment—jusqu'à ce qu'enfin je me sois revu un jour devant une glace de Venise, tel que je m'étais oublié quelques mois auparavant.[1]

This letter is dated 14 May 1867, and *Igitur*, according to Dr. Bonniot, was begun that same year. M. Carrouges wisely remarks that this is not a matter of filiation or influence, but something which is part of the mysterious relationship between man and the universe or the Divinity. Indeed, the image of a bird, and wings—black or white—seems to be one of the

[1] Quoted by Mondor, op. cit., p. 237.

most central images of the relationship between man and the mysteries of the universe—God and Death. The mystic experience, the ascent to God or the coming of God to earth, is associated with wings; it is so in St. John of the Cross, it was so in ancient mythology. The idea of Death is also associated with wings, the wings of the dark angel which transport the soul out of this world. The suggestion that the night of *Igitur*—the Nietzschean night of the death of God—[1] and the night of dæmonic spells of Poe could summon the archetypal images and evolve a similar atmosphere does not seem to me far-fetched, but on the contrary a very plausible one; neither is M. Carrouges' conclusion far-fetched when he points out how artificial *The Raven* sounds in comparison with the undefined oppressive atmosphere of Mallarmé's poem, in which we can feel the tension of a distraught sensitiveness stretching desperately towards its uncreated shadow.

[1] Nietzsche confused the night of unknowing—the night of St. John of the Cross—with the night of the death of God. One has to go through nothingness in order to have an experience of pure Being which is also non-Being; but it is a contradiction in terms to talk of the death of God. There is no death, not even in history, which is only a transitional stage of time and eternity.

CHAPTER IV

The evidence from Mallarmé himself

BAUDELAIRE, Mallarmé, Valéry seem to have vied with one another in their praise for, and discipleship of the Master. Mondor deems it wise to intervene in order to decide once and for all which one of them has the right to hold the incense, and at whom the benign icon is smiling from its eternal silence. Valéry, he says, "croit avec un dandysme seyant que Poe a été sa découverte majeure, mais c'est ici en réalité que s'engage avec son maître vrai et avec soi-même, la confrontation essentielle".[1] Valéry, in a letter to Mallarmé, 20 October 1890, had said about Poe "qu'il est peut-être le plus subtil artiste de ce siècle". There is of course the word 'peut-être' which tempers the force of this sweeping statement, yet obviously Mondor thinks that Mallarmé had seen the light before him, and in fact there is enough evidence to support that view. Mallarmé's first meetings with Poe's work date from 1860, and as early as 1866, in a letter to his friend H. Cazalis about the poem *L'Azur*, Mallarmé says:

> Toutefois plus j'irai plus je serai fidèle à ces sévères idées que m'a léguées mon grand maître Edgar Poe.
> Le poème inouï du *Corbeau* a été ainsi fait. Et l'âme du lecteur jouit absolument comme le poète a voulu qu'elle jouît. Elle ne ressent pas une impression autre que celles sur lesquelles il avait compté.[2]

In the same letter, Mallarmé says about his own poem:

> Je te jure qu'il n'y a pas un mot qui ne m'ait coûté plusieurs heures de recherche, et que le premier mot qui

[1] Op. cit., p. 703.　　　　　[2] Mondor, op. cit., p. 191, N2.

revêt la première idée, outre qu'il tend lui-même à l'effet général du poème, sert encore à préparer le dernier.[1]

Here we have both Mallarmé's and Poe's *art poétique*. In another letter to Cazalis, 14 May 1867, Mallarmé completes the exposition of his views on art:

> Il n'y a que la Beauté;—et elle n'a qu'une expression parfaite—la Poésie. Tout le reste est mensonge excepté pour ceux qui vivent du corps, l'amour, et, cet amour de l'esprit, l'amitié.[2]

Mondor adds this comment: "tant il se rappelait la phrase d'Edgar Poe: 'Je désigne la Beauté comme le domaine de la Poésie.' "[3] He could also have quoted Flaubert, who shared to the full these ideas, who lived for his art, and who believed that there was only one perfect form for each idea, in fact that idea and form were one and the same thing.[4] It is interesting to note here that Laforgue, according to E. Raynaud, "estime que Mallarmé ne relève que de la conscience parnassienne dont il est l'apothéose".[5] Mallarmé, in Huret's interview, underlined better than anybody else what separated him from the Parnassians:

> Je crois, quant au fond, que les jeunes sont plus près de l'idéal poétique que les Parnassiens qui traitent encore leurs sujets à la façon des vieux philosophes et des vieux rhéteurs, en présentant les objets directement. Je pense qu'il faut, au contraire, qu'il n'y ait qu'allusion.[6]

Two excellent examples of the way in which Mallarmé transformed and systematised Poe's imprecise remarks concern two of the main tenets of their art. The first is about

---

[1] Quoted by Mondor, op. cit., p. 65.
[2] Ibid., p. 238.   [3] Ibid., p. 238, *note*.
[4] This belief is old, for already David Hume had reduced to complete identity idea and image or form. This view is shared by F. Coppleston in an essay on David Hume and St. John of the Cross, published in *The Month*, August 1952.
[5] Quoted by Mondor, op. cit., p. 687.   [6] Mallarmé, op. cit., p. 869.

inspiration. Poe, in *The Philosophy of Composition*, says: "Most writers—poets in especial—prefer having it understood that they compose by a species of fine frenzy—an ecstatic intuition—and would probably shudder at letting the public take a peep behind the scenes at the elaborate and vacillating crudities of thought."[1] Poe rather scoffs at inspiration, yet, in the end, he neither denies its existence nor, above all, its possible usefulness. Mallarmé goes much further, he puts it on the index, and proclaims its uselessness:

> Le poète idéal n'est point ce vaste épileptique que l'on nous dépeint échevelé, les yeux hagards, émettant indifféremment et d'un seul jet sous l'*inspiration* de je ne sais quelle Muse bavarde, des vers faciles et incohérents, mais un penseur sérieux qui conçoit fortement et qui entoure ses conceptions d'images hardies et lentement ciselées.[2]

In his notes on *The Raven*,[3] Mallarmé, leaving out the question as to whether *The Philosophy of Composition* was genuine or not, stresses the importance of Poe's principle. He does not quite deny the possibility of inspiration, yet his power to force whatever opinion he examines through the crucible of his own poetic sensibility is such that the very symbol of the raven can become for him that of the poet, tired of the world's agitations, and seeking refuge in the eternal unmoving beauty of art:

> Noir vagabond des nuits hagardes, ce *Corbeau*, si l'on se plaît à tirer du poème une image significative, abjure les ténébreux errements, pour aborder enfin une chambre de beauté, somptueusement et judicieusement ordonnée, et y siéger à jamais.[4]

The other example concerns the power of suggestiveness in poetry, which for Poe lies in the union of poetry and music and

[1] *The Works of Edgar Allan Poe*, edited by J. H. Ingram (A. and C. Black, Edinburgh, 1875), vol. iii, p. 267.
[2] From an article by Mallarmé published in the review *Art*.
[3] Mallarmé, op. cit., p. 230.
[4] Ibid.

in the use of certain devices to produce incantation and atmosphere. But Poe's views are extremely vague. Not so Mallarmé's, who made his clear in his reply to J. Huret's 'Enquête sur l'évolution littéraire', *Echo de Paris*, March 1891:

> *Nommer* un objet, [says Mallarmé] c'est supprimer les trois quarts de la jouissance du poème qui est faite de deviner peu à peu: le *suggérer*, voilà le rêve. C'est le parfait usage de ce mystère que constitue le symbole: évoquer petit à petit un objet pour montrer un état d'âme, ou, inversement, choisir un objet et en dégager un état d'âme par une série de déchiffrements. . . . Il doit y avoir toujours énigme en poésie, et c'est le but de la littérature— il n'y en a pas d'autres—d'évoquer les objets.[1]

In a letter to Cazalis, October 1864, he says:

> Peindre non la chose, mais l'effet qu'elle produit. Le vers ne doit pas se composer de mots, mais d'intentions, et toutes les paroles s'effacent devant les sensations.[2]

This is something precise which indicates analytical powers of a different order from those of Poe, in spite of the very high opinion which Mondor has of Poe's theories: "Relire *La Genèse du Poème* de Poe, c'est remonter à la source d'une poésie dont Baudelaire, Mallarmé et Valéry ont donné des chefs-d'œuvres."[3]

Poe was for Mallarmé "l'âme poétique la plus noble qui jamais vécût".[4] "Ayant appris l'anglais pour mieux lire Poe, je suis parti à vingt ans en Angleterre", he says in a letter to Verlaine.[5] In fact, he had studied English for seven years at least before he heard of Poe, and he wanted to be a teacher of English—but that does not matter: Poe was his ideal. He accepted Baudelaire's picture of his hero, yet at the same time reacted in his comments on Poe's poems against "le suprême

[1] Mallarmé, op. cit., p. 869.
[2] Mondor, op. cit., p. 145.
[3] Ibid., p. 188.
[4] Mallarmé, op. cit., p. 531.
[5] Quoted by Mondor, op. cit., p. 73.

tableau à la Delacroix, moitié réel et moitié moral dont Baudelaire a illustré la traduction des contes".[1] He admits Baudelaire's explanation for Poe's drunkenness—heredity, and also a means "de combattre . . . le vide d'une destinée extraordinaire niée par les circonstances".[2] He took to drink "en victime glorieuse et volontaire . . . afin d'arriver à certaines altitudes spirituelles prescrites mais que la nation dont il est, s'avoue incapable d'atteindre par de légitimes moyens".[3] But Mallarmé reduces the importance of Poe's vice as well as the gap which separates Poe from the America to which he belongs, and insists that "le devoir est de vaincre, et un inéluctable despotisme participe du génie".[4] Far from thinking that Poe led an exceptional life, he thinks that Poe led "l'existence simple et monotone d'homme de lettres".[5] In brief, Mallarmé does what Baudelaire had done before him, he conceives Poe in his own image. This Mallarméan Poe is a very mild character compared with the rebellious, satanic Poe of Baudelaire, and, needless to say, it is the Baudelairian concept which triumphed. Mallarmé was not carried away by his predecessor's enthusiasm, he could see that Poe's doctrine was old, and that his artistic tenets had been fully exploited in countries which had had a dramatic art; he felt that in a country without theatrical traditions like America, Poe applied those principles of dramatic art to lyrical poetry, "fille avérée de la seule inspiration",[6] and obviously not subject to such strict architectural control as dramatic art. In a way, Mallarmé echoes Verlaine, who said about Poe: "Quel naïf, ce malin-là."[7] Yet he undoubtedly approves Poe for having shown that inspiration is not synonymous with disorder and confusion:

A savoir que tout hasard doit être banni de l'œuvre moderne et n'y peut-être que feint; et que l'éternal coup

---

[1] Mallarmé, op. cit., p. 226.   [2] Ibid.
[3] Ibid.   [4] Ibid.   [5] Ibid., p. 227.
[6] Quoted by Mondor, op. cit., p. 230.
[7] Quoted by Lemonnier, op. cit., p. 81.

7

d'aile n'exclut pas un regard lucide scrutant l'espace dévoré par son vol.[1]

Talking about *Hérodiade* in a letter to Cazalis, March 1866, Mallarmé says: "Il me faudra bien quatre hivers encore pour achever cette œuvre, mais j'aurai enfin fait ce que je rêve être un poème digne de Poe et que les siens ne surpasseront pas." [2]

In a letter to his friend Mirbeau, he says: "Je suis heureux que vous ayez goûté Poe, le poète, qui est une mortelle eau de source: peu de poèmes tiennent après le chant de ceux-là, trop rares. . . ." [3]

"Je révère l'opinion de Poe", says Mallarmé, "quel génie pour être un poète", and then, superimposing upon Poe's his own conception of poetry: "L'armature intellectuelle du poème se dissimule et tient—a lieu—dans l'espace qui isole les strophes et parmi le blanc du papier: significatif silence qu'il n'est pas moins beau de composer, que les vers." [4]

He does the same thing in the notes following the translation of *For Annie* where, according to Noulet, he defines his own poetry through that of Poe: "Si j'osais . . . porter un jugement . . . je dirais que la poésie de Poe n'est peut-être jamais autant allée hors de tout ce que nous savons, d'un rythme apaisé et lointain, que dans ce chant." [5]

In the portrait of Poe which contains many of the ideas and images which went to the making of his poem *Tombeau d'Edgar Poe*, Mallarmé says:

> Une piété unique telle enjoint de me représenter le pur entre les Esprits, plutôt et dé préférence à quelqu'un, comme un aérolithe; stellaire, de foudre, projeté des desseins finis humains, très loin de nous contemporairement à qui il éclata en pierreries d'une couronne, pour personne, dans maint siècle d'ici. Il est cette exception, en effet, et le cas littéraire absolu.[6]

[1] Mallarmé, op. cit., p. 230. [2] Quoted by Mondor, op. cit., p. 192.
[3] Ibid., p. 543. [4] Mallarmé, op. cit., p. 872.
[5] Ibid., p. 243. [6] Ibid., p. 531.

"Le cas littéraire absolu", that was the aim of Mallarmé as well as the aim of Flaubert. The prototype which Mallarmé tried to emulate was Poe, and his friends, well aware of his feelings, find no greater praise than to compare him to his hero:

> Tu ne saurais croire quelle profonde impression m'ont causée les vers que tu m'as donnés. Toi seul, Edgar Poe et Baudelaire étiez capables de ce poème qui, comme certains regards de femme, contiennent des mondes de pensées et de sensations.[1]

Mendès, speaking of Mallarmé's beginning in an article in *La Vogue Parisienne*, writes:

> Oh! quelle intelligence exquise et subtile révélaient ces quelques pièces toujours bizarres, souvent parfaites. . . . Edgar Poe eût aimé ce poète nouveau qui étonna Charles Baudelaire.

Edgar Poe, Baudelaire, Mallarmé, the three names constantly recur together: Mallarmé himself once more brought them together in his famous translation of Poe's poems published by Vanier in 1889. The volume is dedicated to Baudelaire:

> A la mémoire de Baudelaire, que la mort seule empêcha d'achever, en traduisant l'ensemble de ces poèmes, le monument magnifique et fraternel dédié par son génie à Edgar Poe.

The Deman edition, published in August 1888, had been dedicated to Manet, who had illustrated the poems for both editions. A brief examination of the introductory remarks and the notes of this work of Mallarmé can only confirm the admiration we all know he had for Poe. In his introductory remarks Mallarmé says: "Ce livre . . . peut passer pour un monument du goût français au génie qui, à l'égal de nos maîtres les plus chers et vénérés, chez nous exerça une

[1] Henri Cazalis, July 1864, quoted in Mallarmé, op. cit., p. 1511.

influence."[1] Further on he describes Poe as "le prince spirituel de cet âge", and repeats Baudelaire's words about Poe: "un des plus grands héros littéraires".[2] Mallarmé shares to the full Poe's feelings that the crowd does not understand innovators in art, and, according to him, it was only because they were

> incommodés par tant de mystère insoluble, qu'ils ont, sous le couvert d'un inutile et retardataire tombeau, roulé une pierre immense, informe, lourde, déprécatoire, comme pour bien boucher l'endroit d'ou s'exhalerait vers le ciel, ainsi qu'une pestilence, la juste revendication d'une existence de Poète par tous interdite.[3]

Further on: "Presque pas un des vingt morceaux qui ne soit en son mode un chef-d'œuvre."[4] "*Ulalume*", he says, "est peut-être le poème le plus original et le plus étrangement suggestif de tous." He quotes Mrs. Sarah Helen Whitman as having said that it was "de tous les poèmes, peut-être le plus imaginatif".[5] *For Annie* is "un miracle poétique".[6] *The Bells*, which he describes as "un démon pour les traducteurs", has "une impalpable richesse" which is bound to get lost in passing from one language to another.[7]

Mallarmé therefore continues and even increases the reverential cult of Poe inaugurated by Baudelaire, a cult which Valéry took up with his earliest poems: "Je chéris en poésie comme en prose, les théories si profondes et si perfidement savantes d'Edgar Poe, je crois à la toute puissance du rythme et surtout de l'épithète suggestive."[8]

Now the wheel has come full circle; certain critics go as far as to assert that Poe practically made Valéry: in a book called *Edgar Poe*, M. Alfred Colling says: "Soit dit sans diminuer en

---

[1] Mallarmé, op. cit., p. 223.
[2] Ibid., p. 225.　　　　　　　　　　[3] Ibid., p. 226.
[4] Ibid., p. 228.　　　　　　　　　　[5] Ibid., p. 235.
[6] Ibid., p. 243.　　　　　　　　　　[7] Ibid., p. 240.
[8] Valéry, aged nineteen, on the occasion of sending some poems to a literary review.

rien l'influence du génial poète qu'est Valéry, mais Poe l'a gratifié du bien sans doute le plus précieux à l'artiste: l'unité de l'esprit." [1] One can see that the adulation for Poe's life and æsthetic theories cannot go further. Yet, leaving out for the moment the problem of the application of Poe's æsthetic theories by Mallarmé, or the influence of Poe's poetry on Mallarmé's, problems which we shall discuss later, one cannot but be struck by the fact that there is not a single instance of Mallarmé saying: "This is one of my poems inspired by Poe", as Eliot, for instance, recognised his debt to Dante in the meditation of *Little Gidding*. Claudel, speaking about Mallarmé, whom he greatly admired, says: "J'étais complètement saisi d'admiration, mais l'admiration ou l'envie de faire la même chose sont deux choses complètement différentes"; [2] and further on in the same book he adds: "Tout être vivant developpe une certaine nature, de même que le gland devient un chêne, on en trouve toujours des traces du moins chez un écrivain authentique, qui se développe lui-même, qui ne doit rien à un travail extérieur, ce que les prophètes hébreux appellent 'le travail de sculpture' . . . et bien c'est ce que font les écrivains ou les poètes qui se fabriquent, pour ainsi dire, du dehors, par le travail de la lime et du marteau." And he goes on to include in that latter category of writers, Valéry and Horace. [3]

---

[1] *Edgar Poe* (Albin Michel, Paris, 1952), p. 238.
[2] Paul Claudel, *Mémoires improvisés* (Gallimard, Paris, 1954), p. 65.
[3] Ibid., p. 200.

CHAPTER V

Edgar Allan Poe's poetry and æsthetics

THE POETRY

BYRON'S reputation on the Continent is admittedly much greater than it is in his native country, yet, even in his own country, he is by no means underestimated; his greatness is fully recognised, his place amongst the best of English poets is assured, and critics ranging from scholars like Sir Herbert Grierson, Mr. Wilson Knight and Sir Maurice Bowra to writers like Peter Quennel, W. H. Auden and Sir Herbert Read recognise the range of his genius and the mastery of his gifts. The problem is very different with Poe. In spite of the fact that Baudelaire, Mallarmé and Valéry hail him as a great poet and sing his praise with impressive enthusiasm and unison, English and American critics, unmindful of the opinions of some of their best poets, grant him at best the title of minor poet. They kindly but firmly suggest that the above-mentioned French poets did not know the subtleties of the English language. Professor Mansell Jones says: "Is there not something of a literary curiosity in the fact that certain French poets—reputed to rank with the most exquisite of their race—should have troubled to adapt so many of Poe's tricks and tags to their purposes, producing, even when crudities are softened, effects which appear to be no more in keeping with the French tradition than their prototypes were with the English?"[1] His assessment of Poe's poetry, on the whole, coincides with that of Mr. Shanks, with one slight note of dissent on the importance of the influence of *Ulalume*. He accepts Mr. Shanks'

[1] Op. cit., p. 51.

description of *To Helen* as "the best poem so uncharacteristic of its author that ever was written",[1] and he agrees with him in his praise of "certain fragments and short poems like *Romance, The Sleeper, Israfel,* and Walter de la Mare points to that remarkable juvenile song—

The bower whereat in dreams I see . . .

In these the characteristic mannerisms are subtly disposed, not hammered home as in those that have made Poe's reputation: *The Raven, The Bells, Annabel Lee, For Annie*".[2]

T. S. Eliot, with his customary generosity, suggests, as we already noted, that "we should be prepared to entertain the possibility that these Frenchmen have seen something in Poe that English-speaking readers have missed".[3] Then, from that background of open-mindedness and humility, he proceeds with a very subtle distinction between Poe's worth as a poet and Poe's effect on the three French poets involved, and presents us with a searching and dialectically dissent-proof appraisal of Poe's poetry and of his influence on Baudelaire, Mallarmé and particularly on Valéry. I shall refer later to his appraisal of Poe's poetry and æsthetics; for the moment I only wish to touch upon the point with which T. S. Eliot concludes his remarks on the relationship between language difficulties and the French poets' appreciation of Poe. After having granted the fact that Baudelaire and Mallarmé knew English imperfectly and Valéry probably not at all, he concludes with these words:

The evidence that the French overrated Poe because of their imperfect knowledge of English remains accordingly purely negative: we can venture no farther than saying that they were not disturbed by weaknesses of which we are very much aware. It does not account for their high opinion of Poe's *thought,* for the value which they attached

[1] *Edgar Allan Poe* (Macmillan, 1937), p. 88.
[2] Professor Mansell Jones, op. cit., p. 51.
[3] *From Poe to Valéry,* p. 7.

to his philosophical and critical exercises. To understand that we must look elsewhere.[1]

Now this is the one point about which I should be inclined to differ somewhat from T. S. Eliot. Like him, I should hesitate to say that the whole foundation of the French poets' uncritical admiration for Poe's work merely rests on language; but I should add that as far as Poe's *thought* is concerned, it rests above all on their ignorance of the poetry of the English poets who preceded and outdistanced Poe in practice, and in the theories which Poe on the whole expounds as his. Coleridge, Keats and Shelley had raced over those slopes along which Poe painfully walks and gleans into home-made sheaves the odd stalks and grains which they had left behind; they had even written long poems so that they could not, like Poe, inveigh against this genre. The French poets' ignorance could partially be ascribed to language difficulties; but where their failure in the knowledge of language seems to me pertinent is with regard to their assessment of Poe's poetry and the special niche they accorded him in the Pantheon of Poetry. It is obvious that their ignorance not only made it possible for them not to be disturbed by weaknesses of the most blatant kind, but also enabled them to see beauty where nobody else but they can see it. Their very incomplete grasp of the English language and poetic traditions made it possible for them to conjure up greatness out of certain poems whose weaknesses are obvious. I am inclined to think that in order to try to assess the poetry of a language one must begin by having been practically born and brought up in that language; if not, all the subtle music and evocational power of the words which make poetry are lost. The poetry of a nation and, in the end, poetry itself is like Penelope's cloth, a work which never ends. Every poet adds his own contribution, his own special way of weaving and of bringing out certain patterns, but he still works

[1] Ibid., pp. 21-2.

on the same old warp and woof which have been used by
others, and he works with threads and strands which are part
of the whole; so that in order to be able to receive the impact
of the mnemonic wealth of the words and the rhythms of a
language, a wealth which is part of the magic of poetry, one
must be fully conversant with the literature of that language.
Such was not the case with Baudelaire, Mallarmé and Valéry
with regard to English and English literature; therefore,
important poets though they were, they could not with
adequate means appraise or assess English poetry. They only
grasp the surface meaning, the ideas, and the images, but never
the poetry itself, the rest is their own creation; but for poets or
poetic minds, the less they understand, the more, in some ways,
they create, and therefore the more they love their creations.

I do not propose to attempt an assessment of Poe's poetry;
that has already been done by various eminent critics to whose
judgments I could only subscribe. These judgments easily tip
the scale against those of Poe's French admirers who, however
great they may have been as poets, "could not have felt the
defects and excesses of his manner as we do".[1] Most English
critics agree that the poems upon which Poe's reputation stands
are not those that they would choose as his best. *The Raven*,
The Bells, *Eulalie* may have delighted Baudelaire, Mallarmé
and amateurs of poetry recitals, but they do not satisfy ears
trained to distinguish between subtle melody and mechanical
devices. To try to say what has already been so well said by
T. S. Eliot, Edward Shanks, Middleton Murry or Professor
Mansell Jones would be out of place, and, above all, out of
season. I shall confine my remarks to a few points which show
possible similarities with, and certainly differences from,
Mallarmé's poetry, and I shall concentrate more fully on the
essays which contain Poe's æsthetics.

On the whole, I find myself more in agreement with T. S.
Eliot and Professor Mansell Jones than with Mr. Shanks. I

[1] Professor Mansell Jones, op. cit., p. 52.

cannot agree with his restrictive remark about the last stanza of the sonnet *To Helen*, neither can I see why this poem is uncharacteristic of Poe. I should on the contrary say that here, Poe's vague music, which generally fades away into inchoate feelings and situations, has the firm substratum of a myth or a legend—a substratum which keeps the harmonies in focus. *For Annie* is, as Professor Mansell Jones suggests, unequal; the diction is slightly forced and artificial. We have here and there vague refractions of *Kubla Khan*, only to be left with a certain amount of frustration, for the words have very little conjuring power and they are too imprecise. *Annabel Lee* suffers from the same flaws, its language, which ought to be direct and simple without puerility, is inflated and precious and does not fit a genre in which both Coleridge and Keats have excelled—the modern ballad. But on the whole, *Dream within a Dream*, *The City under the Sea*, *Tamurlane* and most of *Israfel* are good poetry. With regard to *Ulalume*, I agree with T. S. Eliot that it is "one of his most successful as well as typical poems".[1] Yet I share the very slight reservations suggested by Professor Mansell Jones, who thinks that Poe's characteristic mannerisms are still pronounced in this poem, to which Mr. Shanks attaches *singular* importance (the italics are mine). Mr. Shanks says that

> *Ulalume* is the first great poem of the Symbolist school . . . which must be regarded as a masterpiece of execution, of the adaptation of means to end. . . . But the value of the poem to the reader is precisely in the sensation of spiritual disturbance deepening to dismay and terror. The rhythm, images and phrases by which this sensation is conveyed are as generalised as the medium of music. No one will deny that its mysterious images and phrases, its changing and re-echoing rhymes do gradually produce a single effect in the mind of the reader, culminating in the realisation of an inexplicable but unescapable despair.[2]

[1] *From Poe to Valéry*, p. 13.   [2] *Op. cit.*, p. 98.

All this is true, but the mannerism of Poe is still evident in the third and fourth stanzas with their too obviously precious words; above all, the poem is neither the first nor, least of all, a great symbolist poem—Coleridge and Shelley had done that before; though it is a good poem.

Admittedly Coleridge was not self-consciously striving after the same effects as Poe, although he too had stated that poetry should not be completely understood, and although, with him too, composition and the creation of an atmosphere could be at times extremely wilful, as in the case of *The Ancient Mariner*. As for symbolism, there is a greater wealth of hidden meanings, a greater conjuring and incantatory power in the words of *Kubla Khan*, which was apparently written in a trance-like state, than in the laborious composition of Poe. These remarks are meant to suggest two essential points which I shall elaborate later; the first is that what one may call vertical symbolism, that is to say the apprehension of the invisible world through the visible, is part and parcel of all poetry; and the depth of revelation is in direct ratio to the poetic genius. The second one is that what one may call horizontal symbolism, that is to say equivalences, replacements of one thing or one sensuous apprehension by another, and conscious efforts to create atmosphere by suggestiveness, were part of the whole English romantic poetry from Blake to Shelley, and also of post-romantic poets like Tennyson, writers like Carlyle, and pre-Raphaelites like D. G. Rossetti. Poe's didactic turn of mind had merely tried to transform into dogma practices which were part of poetry; and, to my mind, not the least cause of his insistence on composition was no doubt his lack of inspiration.

POE'S ÆSTHETICS

Poe's æsthetics is contained in the two essays, *The Poetic Principle* and *The Philosophy of Composition*; the third essay, *The Rationale of Verse*, is too concerned with technicalities which only apply to English prosody to offer any possible source of influence to poets who did not write in that language.

The Poetic Principle

The essay begins with a skirmish against the long poem whose existence Poe denies, saying that the words 'long poem' are a contradiction in terms.[1] *Paradise Lost*, for him, is merely a series of minor poems. The idea that a long poem is an imaginative synthesis like a painting, a symphony or a tragedy, does not seem to have occurred to Poe, over-preoccupied with the idea of a poem as being the expression of one single mood or one single emotion. A long poem obviously is the synthesis of many moods and emotions, and it may therefore happen that flat passages are as necessary to it as the Fool is to *Lear*, or dull passages or dull patches of colour to a symphony or a painting: the Alps are a mixture of sharp ridges and high lands and not a single sharp needle resting on air. Happily for posterity, neither Mallarmé nor Valéry, in spite of their faith in Poe's gospel, did accept his views about the long poem—Mallarmé left us *L'Après-midi d'un Faune* and *Hérodiade*, and Valéry *La Jeune Parque* and *Fragments du Narcisse*.

The next point raised by Poe is the problem of didacticism in poetry. One might have thought that Shelley, in his *Defence of Poetry*, had said what could be said on that theme. But one must remember that the Victorian age was the age of moral preoccupations, the age of Matthew Arnold defining literature as a criticism of life. So Poe inveighs against truth in poetry. The trouble is that Poe is not really discussing truth itself but the various means of reaching truth, principally the logical and the poetic which is, in its ways, as coherent as the logical and which, although it may be at variance with it with regard to facts and methods, is never at variance with it with regard to essential principles. The truth of Goethe is also that of Kant;

[1] Coleridge in the *Biographia Literaria*, chapter xiv, p. 290, had already said that "a poem of any length neither can be, nor ought to be all poetry."

the journeys towards it are different. "The demands of Truth are severe. She has no sympathy with the myrtles. All *that* which is so indispensable in Song, is precisely all *that* with which *she* has nothing whatever to do. It is but making her a flaunting paradox to wreathe her in gems and flowers."[1]

Poe's division of things and experiences into *poetical* and truthful is artificial in the extreme, and indicates a repudiation of the fundamental fact that poetry is the revelation of the essence of things, which is their truth and their beauty; that means that poetry is everywhere, in all forms of life and human apprehensions of life. Poe fails to realise that even a purely 'poetic' passage in dramatic or descriptive poetry is part of the essence of character or of the thing described, just as the sun's rays are part of the sun, though the sun may no longer be visible. Poe's conception of poetry underlies the broad division between incomplete reason and sentiments which characterises the Victorian age, and opens the way to all sorts of artifices, mannerisms and posturings which have nothing much to do with poetry.

Finally, we come to Poe's division of the world of mind into *pure intellect*, *taste* and *the moral sense*, a division which is at least as arbitrary as the one which separates truth from beauty. Pure intellect may or may not be considered as part of the essences or mind which embraces the universe, but it certainly has a transcendental quality which makes it different in nature from taste and moral sense, which are essentially historical concepts. The relationship between the workings of these three aspects of mind is so shallow as not to be worth examination. This kind of neat categorising seems to me hardly good enough for an elementary class in civics. The truth is that there are extremely few poets with minds truly capable of philosophising; Coleridge is nearly unique in this kind; next to him I should place T. S. Eliot and Valéry. But when second-rate minds attempt to do so, they can only display a

[1] Poe, op. cit., p. 202.

kind of dialectical skill which could easily be accepted as intellectual profundity by unguarded readers, but which will hardly stand a moment of serious reflection. The watertight compartments in which Poe tries to enclose mildly allegorised Reason, Passion, Beauty, Duty and Truth (the capitals are Poe's) are mere castles upon the sand, or fanciful conventions which could be accepted only if one really wished to play Poe's game. One wonders what is that ghostly Beauty which Poe has stripped of all human attributes such as Passion and Reason, which is truly the whole man. The only passage where Poe repeats something worth repeating or elaborates something worth elaborating is the one containing his definition of the 'poetic feeling' as an attempt to grasp the 'supernal Loveliness' of things: "The struggle to apprehend the supernal Loveliness —this struggle, on the part of souls fittingly constituted—has given to the world all *that* which it (the world) has ever been enabled at once to understand and *to feel* as poetic." [1]

This statement, which places poetry on the metaphysical plane and equates it with the very essence of things which is their truth, contradicts Poe's main argument which aims at leaving truth out of poetry, and is fully supported by the poetry of Coleridge and by the rise towards ethereal beauty of Shelley.

The only point which interests us here is Poe's reference to music and poetry. This point is vital in the problem of influence on Mallarmé; for, as we shall see later, from Mallarmé to Verlaine, all symbolist poets, each one with his private meaning, talked about music. A brief examination of the texts will show that although Poe and Mallarmé used the same word, they talked about very different things and they had in mind very different concepts. This is what Poe says about music in *The Poetic Principle*:

> Contenting myself with the certainty that Music, in its various modes of metre, rhythm and rhyme, is of so vast

[1] Ibid., p. 204.

a moment in Poetry as never to be wisely rejected—is so vitally important an adjunct, that he is simply silly who declines its assistance, I will not now pause to maintain its absolute essentiality. It is in Music perhaps that the soul most nearly attains the great end for which, when inspired by the Poetic Sentiment, it struggles—the creation of supernal Beauty. It *may* be, indeed, that here this sublime end is, now and then, attained in *fact*. We are often made to feel, with a shivering delight, that from an earthly harp are stricken notes which *cannot* have been unfamiliar to the angels. And thus there can be little doubt that in the union of Poetry with Music in its popular sense, we shall find the widest field for the Poetic development. The old Bards and Minnesingers had advantages which we do not possess—and Thomas Moore, singing his own songs, was, in the most legitimate manner, perfecting them as poems.[1]

Next to this passage we should place the end of a letter to B.:

A poem, in my opinion, is opposed to a work of science by having, for its *immediate* object, pleasure, not truth; to romance, by having, for its object, an *indefinite* instead of a *definite* pleasure, being a poem only so far as this object is attained; romance presenting perceptible images with definite, poetry with *in*definite sensations, to which end music is an *essential*, since the comprehension of sweet sound is our most indefinite conception. Music, when combined with a pleasurable idea, is poetry; music, without the idea, is simply music; the idea, without the music, is prose, from its very definitiveness.[2]

One should also examine the following extract contained in *Marginalia* CXCVI, which deals with Poe's archetype of poetry —Tennyson:

I *know* that indefinitiveness is an element of the true music—I mean of the true musical expression. Give to it

[1] Ibid., p. 204.   [2] Ibid., p. 318.

any undue decision—imbue it with any very determinate tone—and you deprive it at once of its ethereal, its ideal, its intrinsic and essential character. You dispel its luxury of dream. You dissolve the atmosphere of the mystic upon which it floats. You exhaust it of its breath of faëry. It now becomes a tangible and easily appreciable idea—a thing of the earth, earthy.[1]

Finally one should read the following, from Poe's letter to James R. Lowell, New York, 2 July 1844:

> I am profoundly excited by music and by some poems—those of Tennyson especially—whom with Keats, Shelley, Coleridge (occasionally) and a few others of like thought and expression, I regard as the sole poets. Music is the perfection of the soul or idea of Poetry. The vagueness of exultation aroused by a sweet air which should be strictly indefinite and never too strongly suggestive is precisely what we should aim at in poetry. Affectation which is thus no blemish.[2]

Let us note the point that "music is the perfection of the soul or idea of Poetry". Could it be also the *Idea* of Mallarmé, that is to say the *essence* coming into existence in poetry? The *Ideas* of Mallarmé, although they are strongly intellectualised, are obtained by negating the real into the ideal source of all things—the logos. One cannot see any difference between the *logos*, the *Idea* of Plato and Idea here mentioned by Poe; the difference lies in the means to reach that *Idea*.[3]

The main point which emerges from these quotations from Poe, is the insistence on the importance of indefiniteness and music in poetry, which for Poe is music "with a pleasurable

[1] Ibid., p. 457.

[2] *Letters of E. A. Poe*, edited by John Ostrom (Harvard University Press), vol. i, pp. 257-8.

[3] Coleridge, echoing Shakespeare, had said: " 'The man that has no music in his soul' can indeed never be a genuine poet. . . . But the sense of musical delight, with the power of producing it, is a gift of the imagination." *Coleridge* (The Nonesuch Press, 1950), p. 255.

idea". To be sure, Poe passes rather too easily from the concept of 'indefinite pleasure' to the more general concept of 'indefiniteness' in music and poetry; but the crux of Poe's remark is that the aim of poetry and music is to cause an indefinite pleasure, in other words a pleasant emotional state whence an experience similar to that of the poet may arise. The suggestion I was trying to bring in before is, that all emotional states are not *ipso facto* pleasant, that therefore, either one chooses to limit poetic experience to states of euphoria only, or one must give to the word emotion a neutral meaning of pleasant and unpleasant, and accept the principle that any causation of emotions, whatever they may be, is pleasant, that is to say, pleases the subject. That may be an acceptable proposition, for, after all, there are people who delight in sorrow. This stress on indefiniteness and vagueness fits within the general idea of 'symbolism' as a term covering forms of literary expression which gained the ascendancy at the end of the nineteenth century and are still very important in our time. We are here very close to the art of Verlaine, yet it is not the same. For Verlaine, poetry was what it was for W. B. Yeats—the song flowing with the fluidity and indefiniteness of music but surging from the heart, and not from the head, as with Poe. Verlaine was artful, even more artful than Poe, but his art consisted in hiding artfulness and not in advertising it as a subject of pride. With Poe one has to refrain from examining closely the machinery if one wishes to enjoy his poetry. He himself said: "To see distinctly the machinery—the wheels and pinions—of any work of art is unquestionably, of itself, a pleasure, but one which we are able to enjoy only just in proportion as we do not enjoy the legitimate effect designed by the artist."[1]

The difference between Poe's attitude and that of Mallarmé towards music is fundamental, and is the very measure of the gap which separates their poetry. Both were aware that

[1] Op. cit., *Marginalia* XIV, p. 356.

music is part of poetry, in fact is perhaps poetry itself, but with a marked difference in depth of appreciation. Baudelaire had the poetic genius, the creative innocence which made him a *voyant* and enabled him to reach the depths of poetry. Like Racine, whose purity of style he emulated, his inspirational start, his initial vision was so intense as to suffuse his whole imagery and to prevent any obtrusive conceptualisation. Mallarmé did not have such gifts, but he had, like Valéry, a remarkable mind; he knew that one could not confuse the inner music, the initial melody, the start and source of the poem with the external music of the words. The unheard music which could be the melody, the rhythmic essence of the feeling or emotion which is the starting force of the poem, Mallarmé defined as "le chant jaillit de source innée, antérieure à un concept, si purement que refléter au dehors mille rythmes d'images".[1] It was that original creative impulse, the ideal music of Plato, which he tried to suggest by extracting the essence of things. Mallarmé aims at conveying through words, used not positively but emptied of their contingent meaning, acting like the last fleeting rays of a star which has since died, the essential aspect of an experience, the *idea* of that experience tapering off towards eternity. Instead of Verlainian imprecision and use of the next best word in order to keep meaning in a state of fluidity, Mallarmé uses words with extreme precision, and he uses them to produce effects of movement. In his poetry there is nothing static, no frescoes or arrested images painted in rich colours and well-defined lines; each poem is essentially a duration which only lasts during the tension of its reading, and as soon as the tension lapses, the poem disappears into the whiteness of the page, which is also the silence of eternity. The words are connected not as intrinsic carriers of meaning but as the links of a chain or the notes of a musical composition; they do not aim at creating a state, they aim at being for the creative mind of the reader an act of transcen-

[1] Mondor, *Propos sur la Poésie* (Edition du Rocher, Paris, 1946), p. 164.

dence, a flickering imitation of the passage from nothingness to being—the nothingness of the white page to the poem.

The problem is different with Poe; the hint at Platonism does not hide the fact that he is above all concerned with external music, the music of the words, and that his conception of the relationship between music and words brings him nearer to Wagner than to anybody else, and after him to Tennyson and Swinburne, but certainly not to Mallarmé. Poe starts from a vague emotion which is at once conceptualised and submitted to the logical objectivity of language, and then he uses the music of the words as a means to counteract that logic or to put the intellect to sleep. He does not allow, or he is unable to allow the initial emotion to reach form unfettered by the intellect; on the contrary, he submits that emotion from the start to concepts of form and expression. His approach is therefore in some ways classical, but as he lacks genius he generally follows the path of the minor poets who have walked that way: he often gets lost in sheer mechanics. The music of the words ought to correspond to the inner music, but it does not; the inspirational impulse having been weak, the intellect has worked from concepts and rules untransmuted by creative innocence. The result is that the music of the words is merely an external attribute conferred upon the poem for a purpose, and it is at times so blatant that it falls into the vulgarity castigated by Aldous Huxley in his essay on 'Vulgarity in Literature'.

The Philosophy of Composition

This essay is a re-hash of *The Poetic Principle*. Its arguments, its inferences about poetry have such an air of mathematical ineluctability about them that it is difficult to accept seriously such demands made upon adult credulity. Since, however, we are concerned with the relationship between these skilfully contrived intellectual recipes on the art of causing æsthetic pleasure and the French poets who took them seriously, we

must examine them with due earnestness. It is needless to stress
once more the vagueness and artificiality of allegorised concepts like Beauty, Passion, etc., or the difficulty of accepting
Poe's neat surgical severance of Intellect from Heart; Voltaire
told Boswell that he was very lucky to know exactly what that
little thing called a soul was; Poe is in that respect like Boswell.
Beauty is for Poe, "excitement or pleasurable elevation of the
soul". Such an excitement is of course here obtained through
words, and words have both an *intellectual* and an *affective*
meaning. They postulate a certain form of truth, they have
indeed to be arrayed in a way which does not completely defy
logic, and they create in the reader certain emotions admixed
and adjuvant with, yet different from the purely æsthetic
emotion. In fact, it is always part of the critic's business to try
to disentangle this kind of Gordian knot. The purely æsthetic
emotion aimed at by Poe is unattainable through words, it
can only be attained, and not always, in music or in pure
mathematics; Stravinski has tried and succeeded in writing
music which does not tell a story or express feelings, but he
did not keep up the effort for long. It is not impossible to
think that a painter like Matisse, with his insistence on harmonies of lines and colours, may have entertained a similar
hope of reaching pure æsthetic emotion in painting, but it
seems to me that colours and forms, apprehended through the
senses, necessarily have emotional and also, to a certain extent,
intellectual connotations—form more than colour, for form
is analysable and can more readily be submitted to a criterion
of intellectual truth. In the end, pure beauty must be confined
to means which are extra-sensorial and are out of the realm of
logic, yet having their own logic and laws which must needs
be related to the most inherent laws of life—rhythm and the
laws of numbers; in brief, to the music of Plato. Here one
must introduce very serious restrictions, for rhythm not only
has deep emotional connotations, but it must also respect, in its
final structure, certain forms of rational truth if it wishes to be

æsthetically satisfying. This rational truth may only be, and to my mind only is, the analytical discovery of certain profound truths which are perennial, but the fact remains that once any truth is analytically known and defined, it becomes part of the great law of æsthetics. Man invents nothing, he can only painfully, slowly discover what is and has always been; but once the discovery is made and has become part of analysis, the laws which form the structure of that thing are a form of truth which can no longer be neglected in æsthetic creations. I hold the same view about words—revelations of the unknown reality and voices of things; once rational man has uncovered certain layers in the meaning of words, these meanings, subject to analyses, acquire a kind of universality which can no longer be neglected without negating the existence of the process of the revelation of knowledge, and therefore of the source itself.

Poe's conclusion that "Beauty of whatever kind, in its supreme development, invariably excites the sensitive soul to tears. Melancholy is thus the most legitimate of all the poetical tones"[1] seems to me to miss the essential quality of that kind of sadness which is metaphysical, and has nothing to do with the human melancholy which he suggests. It is the awareness that beauty transcends time, and is therefore merely a glimpse of a world beyond man's finitude, a glimpse which reveals man's plight and is tinged with sadness at the point when the self, after having merged into the perennial life of the cosmos, returns to solitariness and to the awareness of finitude. But this sadness is not melancholy in the human sense, for it carries with it an aura of metaphysical joy which goes with the power given to man to transcend himself and time. Melancholy comes when the power to feel that kind of joy has died, when the vision fails, when man or the poet like Coleridge or Wordsworth has no other visions; then we have *dejection*—a triumphant gesture in the course of which the sorrow of the

[1] Op. cit., p. 270.

loss of transcendence gives rise once more to transcendence, a gesture which is one of the phœnixes of literature.

The end of the essay is of no particular interest. Poe tells us that once he has carefully selected the length, the tone, the refrain and the theme of the poem, he writes the central stanza which is the high peak towards which the poem should rise, and concludes with these words about versification: "*For centuries, no man, in verse, has ever done, or ever seemed to think of doing, an original thing.* The fact is that originality (unless in minds of very unusual force) is by no means a matter, as some suppose, of impulse or intuition. In general, to be found, it must be elaborately sought, and although a positive merit of the highest class, demands in its attainment less of invention than negation."[1] This is a statement too sweeping to be examined in the context of English literature.

The main point of the essay is that Poe has been expounding his theory of composition, once the poem was written; he tells us what he did, how he did it, but he tells us that, once the thing has been done. At best, this could only be an explanation as to how Poe wrote a particular poem—*The Raven*. The method of composition advocated by Poe ought to have been expounded and known first as a mathematical principle, and then he ought to have written his poem according to the principle enunciated, a principle which ought to be valid for all poems of the same type. In the circumstances, it is only a piece of pragmatism, a compound of what Poe was as a poet, and also of what he would have liked to be, a compound which could not be taken to represent with exactitude the poetic 'personality' of Poe; that personality could only be tentatively deduced by an outsider examining Poe's æsthetics, the poem concerned, and also the other non-quoted samples of his poetry. That Poe was a poet is undeniable, but it is also obvious that he lacked artistic gifts and he knew it; the *Philosophy of Composition* may well be a compensatory attempt to supply

[1] Ibid., p. 274.

what he knew he did not have—the perfect control, the sustained effort towards perfection, the industry, as he says in *Marginalia* LXXI, the quality which made Buffon say: "Le génie est une longue patience." Whatever view one may take, the attempt is certainly revelatory of Poe's personality and preoccupations as much as were Flaubert's arguments and insistence on style.

Supposing that one took the *Philosophy of Composition* seriously, one could hardly repress a keen urge to see how these clear-cut, skilfully enunciated principles have been put into practice in *The Raven*. A brief examination of this poem will show us that either something went wrong with the blue-print or, what is more probable, the blue-print and the poem are two very different things. One could be the make-believe, the hoax or the wish-fulfilment, the other the real thing with all the traits and failings of the poet Poe, failings and traits which will show the distance which separates it from any one of Mallarmé's poems. The short preface to the book where we find the poem, ends with a sentence which contradicts a great deal of *The Philosophy of Composition*: "With me poetry has been not a purpose, but a passion; and the passions should be held in reverence; they must not—they cannot at will be excited, with an eye to the paltry compensations, or the more paltry commendations, of mankind." [1] Here he says that he cannot be excited at will, while in *The Philosophy of Composition* passion is banned and everything is under perfect control. Still, let us not dwell on Poe's contradictions, they are no more important than those of the average poet, they are part of poetry.

It is difficult to believe that the composition of *The Raven* was as meticulous and deliberate as is purported by Poe's essay. The numerous weaknesses of the poem rather suggest a carelessness and complacency which could only be ascribed to hasty work. The main flaw of the poem, which is the true foundation of Poe's insistence on the great part played by

[1] Op. cit., p. vii.

deliberate choice and consciousness of effort, rests upon his wilful decision to deal with an experience which he had not imaginatively lived. The reason why he chose such an experience could be both inherent to his personality, and also wilful in order to fit his character. He may have been intuitively attracted by that theme and he may also have thought that it was an attractive theme; it is difficult to determine the relationship between something which gives us pleasure and something which we think ought to please us; at one point the intellect intervenes to order our feelings according to a concept; yet the predisposition to such a concept cannot but be affective. Anyhow, it seems to me clear that Poe, in writing *The Raven*, wrote beyond his experience, and his wilfulness in the choice of the theme was not backed by pertinacity of purpose and sustained effort in composition. *The Raven* remains unconvincing, and its attempts at seriousness are marred by the laborious choice of 'poetical' words, by jingle rhyme and by the comic effect of triple and quadruple repetition of these rhymes. The poem is above all a 'composition', something made with all the tricks of the trade. The abundance of epithets, the repetition of facile alliterations and rhymes in 'ing' imply histrionic tendencies, lack of taste and lack of fastidiousness. The redundancies in ideas, the contradictions in meaning show that Poe was mainly concerned with cheap effects and not with certain fundamental problems of poetry. The raven is, as T. S. Eliot has pointed out, both stately and ungainly, Lenore is named and declared nameless; above all, the words do not image, they are merely chosen for their sound, for their superficial beauty. There is hardly any simile or metaphor; and in spite of Poe's objection to narrative poetry, *The Raven* is first and foremost a short story in verse. It is a very dramatic one, told with skill, but which has nothing much to do with pure poetry as propounded by Poe. The process which consists in beginning with the climax or the dénouement does not apply to non-narrative poetry, which is above all a journey of discovery. In *The Raven*, the subject dominates the poem; there is of course a certain poetic feeling, but there is no reality behind the poem, no organic structure and no movement; there is only a kind of one-way flow along a well-known bed of standard sentiments with a complete reliance on certain key-words for their 'poetical' value, or for their obvious connection with the atmosphere which the poet wants to create.

If we examine another essay of Poe, *Eureka*, which so deeply impressed Valéry, we shall see how Poe applies to a prose work meant to carry a certain amount of intellectual knowledge, methods of composition which are similar to the ones he uses for poetry and which produce similar results. *Eureka* is neither a good account of the natural history of the universe, nor a poem with imaginative consistency and truth. It is neither something which could be accepted as scientific truth nor a subjective form of truth about the universe and about man's relation to that universe and to its essence. It is neither truly discursive knowledge nor imaginative knowledge about the universe as Poe genuinely sees it and apprehends it. It is merely about how Poe would like it to be thought that he apprehends the universe, and therefore, as is so often the case with Poe, it is something written for an audience, for readers whom he wishes to convince of something, but it is not written with a view to imparting to them a deeply felt experience. I cannot see the reason for Valéry's praise or for his belief that one could apprehend the beauty and truth of this essay by entering into the spirit of the author. The vital point surely is that in order that such an operation might be possible, the work of art (if one can use such a term for *Eureka*) needs to have been objectified, that is to say given a life of its own as the embodiment through form of an experience which, because it has found in every one of its aspects its true expression, has acquired some kind of organic life. Yet in this case, as in the case of a good deal of Poe's poetry, one cannot but be made aware of the pose, of the set attitude in which the author would like to be descried by his readers; one can see that he does not work with genuine, individual emotions whose truth could lead to the universal, but with conceptualised emotions which are hopelessly bogged half-way between the contingent and the universal or essential. There cannot be any possibility of movement if one starts from the middle of the process and if one endeavours to use concepts as part of imaginative truth. Poe's confessions about the origin of *The Raven* emphasise this point; he explicitly started from an abstraction, an idea of terror, and he proceeded with method and undeniable earnestness in the task of trying to create the emotion which he and the audience ought to feel at the thought of such an abstraction. His aim was to produce an effect, his emotions are therefore wilfully coloured by the idea he wishes to convey. The result is idea-emotion and a kind of rhetoric which is sometimes successful but which most of the time is simply hollow. The words in this case are used as instruments to create certain effects, and at times as isolated jewels. For Mallarmé, as we shall see, the words are part of the whole, they must be integrated in the verse: "Si véritablement les pierres précieuses dont on se pare ne manifestent pas un état d'âme, c'est indûment qu'on s'en pare."

According to Poe's essay *The Rationale of Verse*, it is the melody which matters most. Poetry was for Poe essentially composition, therefore versification; words were counters with a certain sound and a certain suggestive power. Yet, as T. S. Eliot has said, and other critics have echoed him, the rhythms of Poe remain, they strike one at a primitive level, and some of them are unforgettable. "Furthermore," says Montgomery Belgion, "not only do some at least of those poems become embedded in the memory and continue to give pleasure whenever they are recalled; there is something else and it has to be noted."[1] That something else is, that beyond

[1] Op. cit., p. 61.
Huret, J. Enquete sur l'evolution literare cheysentie, 1891.

the superficial failings lies this rhythmic power of striking at a primitive level of receptivity outlined by T. S. Eliot:

> The effect of Poe's versification is immediate and un-developing; it is probably much the same for the sensitive schoolboy and for the ripe mind and cultivated ear. In this unchanging immediacy, it partakes perhaps more of the character of very good *verse* than of poetry—but that is to start a hare which I have no intention of following here, for it is, I am sure, 'poetry' and not 'verse'. It has the effect of an incantation which, because of its very crudity, stirs the feelings at a deep and almost primitive level. But, in his choice of the word which has the right *sound*, Poe is by no means careful that it should have also the right *sense*. I will give one comparison of uses of the same word by Poe and by Tennyson—who, of all English poets since Milton, had probably the most accurate and fastidious appreciation of the sound of syllables.[1]

"I am not sure", said Poe, "that Tennyson is not the greatest of poets."[2] If he had said the greatest of craftsmen he would certainly have been nearer the truth. There is no doubt that Tennyson was Poe's great admiration, and there is even less doubt that Poe is, to my mind at least, in more than one way, a minor Tennyson with many of the defects of Tennyson's great qualities. Both poets grew up in the same atmosphere of transition, the atmosphere in which the spent force of romanticism had come to rest in the 'calm coves' of Victorianism. At that moment, spiritual and material instability begins to die down, order begins to reign, prosperity to appear; the wave of imaginative exuberance is at a low ebb. In spite of the prevalence of strong idealist currents, like that represented by Carlyle and Ruskin, which show that Blake's tradition is not dead, and in spite of the fact that Wordsworth is still alive, the

---

[1] *From Poe to Valéry*, p. 13.
[2] Op. cit., *Marginalia* CXCVI, p. 456.

scientific spirit is in the ascendancy. Utilitarianism, positivism and realism gain ground, and with them we witness in the arts an effort towards objectivity, control and perfection of expression; in fact, the new æstheticism is being born. It comes to light with Tennyson and it will be developed by the pre-Raphaelites, through their transformation of Keats' Beauty into artificial beauty. With Tennyson, we turn from the luxuriance, depth and intensity of Wordsworth, Coleridge, Shelley and Keats, to Popean love of order and artfulness which adorn nature and human feelings with all the graces of the mind. Everything is toned down, sieved through the personality of the poet, a personality which is urbane, but limited in range, nobly moralising, but whose imagination is so deprived of the sense of mystery as to make the poet of *In Memoriam* say about his friend who had died before he was a Member of Parliament that he must be serving now "in such great offices as suit the full-grown energies of Heaven". We move far away from Wordsworth's view that poetry is everywhere in things, whether simple or complex, towards the belief that poetry and beauty are only part of an atmosphere of remote legends and distant past, of certain themes and subjects, and that it can only be expressed in a style which is more concerned with its conscious beauty than with essential truth. In this age of rising scientific rationalism, poetry tends to be more and more the unreal, the remote world of the past; all feelings and actions are refined by a transposition of atmosphere so that reality may remain the privilege of reason—the reason of history—which is more and more worshipped and which therefore must not suffer any admixture with poetry or sentiments, which are considered unworthy of its status. We have only to think of the response of that age to Browning's more intense and more intellectually complex poetry. Style tends to become an end in itself, and we pass easily from the mannerisms of Tennyson to the mechanicalness of Poe, from the mellifluousness of the master to the jingles of the enthusiastic admirer. Tennyson treated romantic themes with consciously studied mastery, as the sources of a music echoing moods in measured movements and pure melodies embodied in an extraordinary variety of metres. Lacking in the kind of inspiration and imagination which could transport the great poets out of the world, he was not concerned with a Goethean "exact sensuous apprehension of things", but with a sonorous equivalence of these things and moods; he remained on the surface. He was shallow; Poe was even more shallow, and with lesser gifts as a poet. Tennyson's growing æstheticism becomes with Poe the dogma which replaces his absent inspiration and poetic gifts; the ingredients of poetry—theme, style, etc.—tend to become poetry itself. Poe despised what he certainly did not understand; he called the Lake Poets—Wordsworth, Coleridge, Southey—the metaphysicals. His famous letter to B.[1] shows how completely he misunderstood Wordsworth and Coleridge and, at the same time, poetry. He felt that these poets' pre-occupations with thought were completely alien to poetry, yet he quotes Aristotle, yet he talks elsewhere about beauty divorced from the essences as if it were a mere dialectical concept, and in a way which shows a very incomplete aware-ness of the deep intuitive insight of Keats and of the extra-ordinary mind of Coleridge; in spite of his shafts directed at intellect, in the end few poets lost more than Poe in trying to mix science and poetry.

On the whole, the poetry and the ideas of Poe belong to his age, and if one examines them, not with a microscope—which is unnecessary—but with the naked eye, one can easily see that the traces which he has left behind him are parts of the trails left by his contemporaries; they are not by any means deep-sea surges which ripple slowly from continent to conti-nent, they are merely the surf in the wake of vast swells caused by forces much greater than his. The most important fact of Poe's inheritance is his insistence on control and construction

[1] Op. cit., pp. 314–15.

115

—two tenets which were essentially derived from short-story writing and from his love of mathematics. Valéry, with his love of composition and mathematics, has done more than anybody else to uphold these two aspects of Poe's æsthetics. Poe's longer poems, in spite of his denial, are to a large extent narrative. Symbolist poetry is not narrative, it is a succession of psychological states on a given theme, but the poem whose effect is above all suggestive and not descriptive is built up in a very controlled and careful way. Inspiration there is, as is the case with post-symbolists like Eliot and Yeats, or in the great musical compositions, but inspiration making, as in music, full use of all the technical assets and skill required to weld together complex aspects of the poet's psyche. The aim is to transmute experience, not in terms of a story, simple object-references or descriptive language, but in terms of successive inner states conveyed by symbols and referential, suggestive language, handled in a way which is analogical to a musical composition. Words are used not to describe the phenomenon, but to suggest the noumenon, the very idea of the thing, the point where apprehension becomes music towards silence. The metaphor is essentially a reference to the absolute, the image is the vision of an emotional and intellectual complex which in the timeless moment can reach from the sensuous picture to its source or idea, which is in eternity.

CHAPTER VI

Mallarmé's poetry and æsthetics

POETIC DICTION IN MALLARMÉ

THIBAUDET sees in Mallarmé a continuation of the Parnasse: "Mallarmé eût voulu, en vieux Parnassien, inspirer la probité du métier littéraire." [1]

That Mallarmé had a great deal in common with the Parnassians seems to me undeniable. He had, like most of them, an aristocratic personality which believed in an artistic élite and in a select language perfectly controlled; he disdained the mob and popularity. He could have said, like Leconte de Lisle:

> Je ne livrerai pas ma vie à tes huées,
> Je ne danserai pas sur ton tréteau banal
> Avec tes histrions et tes prostituées.

He had in him the haughty disdain of vulgarity and sentimentality which we find in Vigny—the Vigny of *La Mort du Loup*; or in Baudelaire—the Baudelaire of "Je hais le mouvement qui déplace les lignes". Mallarmé's insistence on quality and control is part of the reaction against quantity and the search for sensation of the romantics. His insistence on purity in poetry and perfection of form is shared by the Parnassians and Baudelaire, and is the emanation of an age which was tired with the exuberance of sentiments which had produced so many samples of egomania and exhibitionism in poetry. Mallarmé tried to restore the poet in his pristine rôle of creator using each word as if it had been newly minted. In that respect he goes beyond the Parnassians, even beyond Flaubert, to rejoin Rimbaud and his cabalistic faith in the word. After Mallarmé, after Flaubert,

[1] Op. cit., p. 360.

117

the masterpiece of literature is self-creative language; the distinction between content and form has vanished, and the work of art, which before admitted a conscious attempt to bring together the idea or the concept and its form—language —has become now the systematic exploitation of all the inherent properties of language. In brief, the idea is the form, language is all, it is the great memory which contains all human knowledge, and just as the *logos* brought revelation into time, language can, through the medium of the poet, bring eternity into time. The words have acquired transcendence; the æsthetico-religiosity of Matthew Arnold, the loss of faith or, if one wishes, the search for a new faith have led man into pure subjectivity, and into the acceptance of a form of transcendence born from the demiurgic power of the words. We have here a flight from the Hegelian belief in the overriding importance of society over the individual, towards a belief which sees the individual, not as an insignificant component atom of the whole, but on the contrary, as the atom which has in itself the mystery of the whole—the microcosm which is the image of the macrocosm and has the means to recapture, in the state of pure subjectivity, the mystery of creation. We have therefore a re-emergence of Rousseau's belief in the timeless moment which fuses into ecstatic oneness, subjectivity and pure sensation, the sensitive soul and the universe; the pure self becomes the measure of being and the source of all knowledge:

J'aspire au moment où, délivré des entraves du corps, je serai moi sans contradiction, sans partage, et n'aurai besoin que de moi pour être heureux.[1]

and:

Le contemplateur . . . se perd avec une délicieuse ivresse dans l'immensité de ce beau système avec lequel il se sent indentifié. Alors tous les objets particuliers lui échappent; il ne voit et ne sent rien que dans le tout.[2]

[1] *Emile*, p. 346.   [2] *Rêveries*, p. 65.

We do not have a return to Rousseau's ecstatic pantheism, but we have the belief which was also his and which will be stated clearly by Husserl that pure subjectivity is the absolute—the great whole, and that the phenomenal world is only a means to suggest and to travel towards pure subjectivity and absolute knowledge.

Mallarmé stands at the hinge of that transitional period; he is part of the Parnasse, yet he also prolongs it; he is, indeed, in spite of what Gide said, an 'initiateur': "Ne pouvant écouter nul autre, on ne sut point voir en lui le représentant dernier et le plus parfait du Parnasse, son sommet, son accomplissement et sa consommation; on y vit un initiateur."[1] He was not only a 'purist' like the Parnassians, but as Rémy de Gourmont says: "Mallarmé a contribué à donner à la littérature le goût du mystère, du vague, du délicieux imprécis." [2] One can easily see that Mallarmé's views were closely related to those of many poets of his generation and of those who preceded it. Thibaudet traces even further some of Mallarmé's roots; he says: "Il prolonge un courant contre lequel l'art classique a formé ses barrages, celui de la préciosité."[3] And he draws a brief parallel between Mallarmé's 'purism' and Jansenist asceticism. There is no doubt that purism was for Mallarmé a kind of religion. Mallarmé was precious and wilfully recherché in language and in behaviour, and that, as Noulet says, is due to the fact that:

> La supériorité de Mallarmé, c'est qu'il croit, non à sa mission comme Hugo, mais à une sanctification. L'acuité de l'existence poétique, il l'éprouvait comme un état plus pur et si puissant qu'il ne sentait plus la nécessité de passer de l'état à l'acte. Son dialogue intérieur avec la poésie était si continu qu'il n'eut plus besoin de paroles.[4]

Mallarmé had only one constant preoccupation—his art—for which, like Flaubert, he lived.

[1] Quoted by Thibaudet, op. cit., p. 362.   [2] Ibid., p. 366.
[3] Op. cit., p. 371.   [4] Ibid., p. 316–17.

Le passage du songe à la parole occupe cette vie infiniment simple de toutes les combinaisons d'une intelligence
étrangement déliée.[1]

Let us see now what is meant by Mallarmé's purism.

L'art poétique de Mallarmé [says Thibaudet] consiste à purifier le vers non comme on l'a cru de sa signification réelle, mais de ce qui dans cette signification appartient
à la phrase, à la prose. . . . Son idéal serait des caractères
juxtaposés, sans phrase, ni grammaire, où l'ordre syntaxique ne déformerait pas la pureté des mots, où l'esprit
de la syntaxe serait chez le lecteur, non la réalité de la
syntaxe sur le papier. [2]

For Mallarmé, what counts is not the word in isolation but the
line which can express the Idea.

Le vers qui de plusieurs vocables refait un mot total,
neuf, étranger à la langue et comme incantatone achève cet
isolement de la parole.[3]

The art of the poet works not on the isolated words, but on
their arrangement which forms the line or the whole poem;
the words do not exist except as part of the whole. Thence the
importance of form, form being the means to reach the Idea
which for Flaubert was unique and for Mallarmé a return to
the absolute. Each word has therefore to be weighed and to be
used in a way which could give it its original meaning, so as
to reach, through the line or the whole poem, the Idea.

Dans notre langue, [says Mallarmé] les vers ne vont que
par deux ou à plusieurs, en raison de leur accord final, soit
la loi mystérieuse de la Rime qui se révèle avec la fonction
de gardienne et d'empêcher qu'entre tous un usurpe ou ne
demeure péremptoirement.[4]

[1] Valéry, *Variété II*.   [2] Op. cit., p. 183.
[3] Mallarmé, op. cit., p. 368.   [4] Ibid., p. 333.

Two points emerge from this quotation: first, the fact that Mallarmé sees lines as part of the whole and never in isolation; second, the importance of the rhyme as a means to sustain the poetic movement and to knit together the various lines; Mallarmé had a Parnassian respect for rhyme. Rhyme has a kind of deterministic influence on the line. Banville, whom, according to Thibaudet,[1] Mallarmé recognised as one of his heroes, thought that the influence of the rhyme was felt from the very first syllable of the line. In the end, rhyme is to the line what determinism is to liberty—a necessary foundation; at the same time rhyme creates an unfavourable climate for the birth of the isolated, beautiful line.

Mallarmé's use of rhyme continues a tradition as old as French poetry. The use he makes of it is neither exactly that of his predecessors, nor that of Poe, who was above all concerned with rhyme as a means to multiply pleasure.[2] Rhymes in Mallarmé are rich, jewel-like, but they are never trite and noisy as in Poe; they are extremely important, they are an integral part of the structure of the poem, but they are neither an adornment nor, even less, are they a gaudy apparel which the line wears in order to attract attention. Together with rhymes used in a masterly way, we have assonances and alliterations; they are harmonious, subtle and they are the product of a very fastidious and refined sensibility. The sonnet which begins 'Le vierge, le vivace . . .' is a masterpiece in harmonisation of sounds. Needless to say that with such masters as Racine or Victor Hugo, who had made full use of repetition, it would be rather idle to try to discover foreign influences in traits which were part and parcel of French poetry. Mallarmé knew and admired Hugo, who had greatly increased the resources of the alexandrine. His main contribution had been the *enjambement*[3] which breaks the coincidence between

[1] Op. cit., p. 191.
[2] Poe, op. cit., p. 443.
[3] Hugo admired Shakespeare and may have been deeply struck by the rich use of the overflowing line in Shakespeare's later plays.

meaning and rhyme and attenuates its mechanical effect, in the same way as alliterations and assonances attenuate its sound value. Mallarmé and Verlaine admired the old alexandrine too much to cast it aside; indeed, for Mallarmé it still remains 'le grand vers', the one which is so revered that one might perhaps hesitate to use it for all occasions, for one must not disturb without serious reasons 'les échos vénérables'. Mallarmé therefore sought to enhance the beauty of the alexandrine; and his main contribution, together with that of Verlaine, is not only the overflow forward but also backward; so that, with the meaning pervading many lines, the alexandrine acquires a sinuousness whose main vertebrae are the rhymes, but whose meaning spreads over many lines and sometimes over the whole poem. Mallarmé uses the overflow in a unique way, in order to throw into relief facets of meanings or words which have a particular value for a poem, so that two adjectives, or a substantive and its adjective, often find themselves very far one from the other. Victor Hugo and the Parnassians had not freed themselves from the old classical rhetoric. Mallarmé and Verlaine break up the old classical phrase which becomes more plastic, less obvious and more difficult to follow in its subterranean meanings. Mallarmé achieves this result mostly by the subtleness of his pauses and the overflow of the lines, Verlaine by harmonious repetitions.

Mallarmé was not a revolutionary for revolution's sake, he respected the traditions of the language, he did not believe in the necessity for every poet to have his own prosody; "why not a new spelling?" he said, thinking this a joke worthy of preface writers. When he arrived in Oxford for his lecture on 'La Musique et les Lettres', the first words he uttered to an audience waiting to hear his message were:

J'apporte en effet des nouvelles. Les plus surprenantes. Même cas ne se vit encore.

On a touché au vers.[1]

[1] Op. cit., p. 643.

That, for Mallarmé, was the most important news he had to deliver, for "le vers est tout, dès qu'on écrit".[1] Then he went on to explain that the *vers libre*, the new discovery, was nothing but the result of the breaking up, by the romantics, of the alexandrine which, according to Mallarmé, "restera, aux grandes cérémonies".[2] He saw clearly the causes of the appearance of free verse: the romantics had prepared the way with the importance of poetic prose, and for Mallarmé *vers libre* is "prose à coupe méditée";[3] together with it, one must take into account the preponderance of music at the end of the nineteenth century and, above all, the reaction against the failings of the Parnassians who had overstressed the visual aspect of poetry. In a well-known note at the end of 'La Musique et les Lettres', Mallarmé explains the main responsibility of the Parnasse: "il instaura le vers énoncé seul sans participation d'un souffle préalable chez le lecteur ou mû par la vertu de la place et de la dimension des mots."[4] It had become an empty mechanism, and Mallarmé concludes his note by saying: "Au vers impersonnel ou pur s'adaptera l'instinct qui dégage, du monde, un chant, pour en illuminer le rythme fondamental et rejette, vain, le résidu."[5]

Mallarmé saw the weaknesses of the Parnassians, and the remedy, for him, did not lie in repudiating the traditional form, but on the contrary in perfecting it, and in trying to extract new beauty from it. So he concentrated more and more on form, and in later days he wrote mostly sonnets. Like the Parnassians, he wrote for the eye, but for different reasons. His poetry does not strike any hieratic poses meant to be admired at leisure; no, his poetry, intricate, nimble, arabesque-like, has to be seen so that its movement may be grasped. The ear cannot follow it without the eye.

Whether he writes in prose or in verse, Mallarmé, who shared Flaubert's preoccupation with the Idea, is the opposite

[1] Ibid., p. 644.   [2] Ibid.
[3] Ibid., p. 655.   [4] Ibid.   [5] Ibid.

of Flaubert in that his writings are completely anti-rhetorical, they are not meant to be read aloud, to be passed through the *gueuloir*. Jules de Goncourt found in *Salammbô* "une trop belle syntaxe, une syntaxe à l'usage des vieux universitaires fleg-matiques, une syntaxe d'oraison funèbre, sans une de ces audaces de tour, de ces sveltes élégances, de ces virevoltes nerveuses dans lesquelles vibre la modernité du style con-temporain".[1] Mallarmé's prose and poetry are meant to be followed with the care and anxiety with which one follows the nimble steps of a ballet-dancer. His prose follows the apparent ease and carefree way of the development of thought; it is not arrayed according to rhetoric and grammar, it is swift irrational language, which the reader can penetrate and follow if he realises that he has to make the necessary effort to recapture the mental process of the creative mind who wishes him not to accept a given picture, but to make a journey similar to the one made by the poet himself. This boils down to the belief that knowledge is a creative act. Mallarmé suggested that verse only differs from prose by metrical rhythm. "L'acte poétique consiste à voir soudain qu'une idée se fractionne en un nombre de motifs égaux par valeur et à les grouper."[2] Whether in prose or in verse, Mallarmé follows not the order of logic, but the order of sensations; he does not follow the natural order of words, but proceeds by cumulative effects and not through logical developments.[3] He refuses to make his inner meanings fit into the rhetoric of language, and so he uses French as an inflected and synthetic language, as if it were German, Chinese or Latin which Mallarmé knew. As we have seen in the previous chapter, Noulet saw in this attitude an influence from his translations of Poe and from his knowledge of English. This must remain a point difficult to settle. True enough, the knowledge of an inflected language—yet English

[1] *Journal* des Goncourt, vol. i, p. 374.
[2] Mallarmé, op. cit., p. 365.
[3] The only other poet who has been as exacting as Mallarmé over form, and is as concerned as he is with language, is Gerard Manley Hopkins.

is not such a language, though it is more inflected than French
—could suggest the kind of meanings one could reach through
such a medium, but the essential point is, that in order to search,
one must be both so inclined and also have the means to do so.
If it were not so, the inference would lead us to untenable
generalisations. Mallarmé's means are beyond doubt; and
above all, his aims, as Noulet so wisely points out, were stated
in an essay called 'L'Art pour tous' which was written before
Mallarmé was twenty and which was published in *L'Artiste*,
15 September 1862. That text, written before he went to
England, contains the essence of his views about poetry, views
which he constantly sought to perfect and to embody in his
writings. We shall see later the importance of that text; for
the moment let us merely note the time of its appearance in
Mallarmé's life, and also its last sentence:

> O poètes, vous avez toujours été orgueilleux; soyez plus,
> devenez dédaigneux.[1]

Vigny and Leconte de Lisle obviously were not very far away.
A final point which one must note here is that if Mallarmé's
poetry was meant to be read with the eyes, Poe's poetry was
certainly meant to be read aloud. Mallarmé, says Thibaudet,
"est à l'opposé du génie oratoire".[2] He was against writing as
one speaks; and even his conversation was less a carefully
developed argument than a way of thinking aloud, for he did
not so much take up a subject and analyse it, as surround it
and, like a conjuror, annihilate it. Mallarmé writes as one
thinks and not as one talks, he writes to communicate thoughts
and visions and not gestures; and even punctuation is part of
the music of the line, indicating the movement of the journey
towards silence and the mystery of writing. Thence, in the
end, his faith in *le livre*, *le livre* being, as Thibaudet says, "non
un substitut de la parole mais un absolu, une part infiniment

[1] Mallarmé, op. cit., p. 260.
[2] Op. cit., p. 282.

épurée: la parole n'en est que l'essai, le balbutiement, elle va vers lui à son achèvement, à sa fleur".[1]

"L'œuvre pure", says Mallarmé, "implique la disparition élocutoire du poète qui cède l'initiative aux mots."[2] Mallarmé dreamt of a book in which the disposition of the lines, the blanks on the page, everything, would play a part. "Son esthétique du livre, celle qu'il essaiera dans *Un Coup de Dés*, je ne sais pas si elle ne lui est pas venue en partie de ses méditations sur la Danse."[3] The white page is the stage, the lines and words are the ballet; the dancer is not a man or a woman but, just like the words, a symbol, an emblem of something—the dancer suggests what words would find it difficult to say: "un poème dégagé de tout appareil de scribe".[4] Dance is for Mallarmé "la forme théâtrale par excellence", it is the ideal of his poetry as it was going to be that of Valéry, it is a synthesis of poetry and music.[5] Poetry propagates itself by music and dance which are only the reflections emanating from the diamond, from the supreme art which is poetry. Mallarmé's poetry combines, like ballet, movement and arabesque; or like Chinese poetry, the auditory with the visual element of ideograms. The images of Mallarmé's poetry are always fleeting like the vision of the *Faune*; the dominant colour is white—swans, snow—all symbolising absence. His substantives are more important than verbs, for they are more indefinite, and verbs are often used as substantives. He uses language to get out of Time, and he always tries to get out of language in his pursuit of the absolute, arrogating to himself, as Villiers de L'Isle-Adam did, the right to recreate everything. He uses language as music or he replaces it by the architecture of the printed page, as in *Un Coup de Dés*.[6]

[1] Op. cit., p. 283. [2] Ibid., p. 366.
[3] Thibaudet, op. cit., p. 285. [4] Mallarmé, op. cit., p. 304.
[5] "Every kind of language is in this way a specialised form of bodily gesture, and in this sense it may be said that the dance is the mother of all languages" (R. G. Collingwood, *The Principles of Art*, p. 243).
[6] An example which Apollinaire, Claudel and Cummings were going to follow.

Le livre, expansion totale de la lettre, doit d'elle tirer, directement, une mobilité et spacieux, par correspondance, instituer un jeu, on ne sait, qui confirme la fiction.[1]

Mallarmé, says Thibaudet,[2] hesitated between *le livre*—an end in itself—and the book as a means of suggestion and movement as used in the theatre. In the first case the book is in the end silence, in the second the movement—the poetry is the means to reach silence—the absolute.

POETRY AND MUSIC

The relationship between poetry and music is an ever-present factor in the poetry of all the poets who, from Verlaine and Mallarmé to Valéry, are described as symbolists or post-symbolists. We have previously seen what was Poe's literary conception of music; it was, above all, indefiniteness. Mallarmé's conception of music is something different; he probably was very impressed by Poe's insistence on music, but as he lived in a different age, and as his leanings were different, the roots of Mallarmé's conception of music are different from those of Poe and connect him with a tradition which goes back to Plato. The pre-eminent position of music in the liberal arts is based on the position given to music by Plato, and, after him, by the Pythagoreans and by Aristotle. The metaphysical meaning of music in the construction of the universe and of man, and its moral and political value in the education of the citizen are to be found in *The Republic* and in *The Timaeus*. Quintilian[3] deals with that theme, which could be summed up as follows: Plato and the Pythagoreans teach us that the universe is musically constructed and that the human soul is similarly formed. Plato required music from his ideal statesmen and Lycurgus approved of it. Formerly the art of music and the art of letters were united, some even subordinating grammar

---

[1] Mallarmé, op. cit., p. 380.   [2] Op. cit., p. 292.
[3] Quintilian, *Institutio Oratoria*, Book I, ch. 10, paras. 9–20.

to music. The neo-Platonists believed that states of mind were controlled by music, and that everything—animals and human beings—shared in the world's soul which gives motion and sound to the spheres. They believed that, although men were not physically capable of hearing the spheres' music, they responded to music because of their memory of celestial music. They conceived Heaven as the archetype of musical instruments, tuned to make musical accompaniments to the hymns sung in honour of the Father of all things. The superiority of theoretical over practical music is stressed by Boethius and the early Church Fathers, and it combines with Plato's concept—that true music is philosophy—in order to produce the important extension that internal song is more valuable than audible music. This is the central point in the legend of St. Cecilia who, at her wedding, sang internally to God alone.

Here we have the equation of music with silence which is also the Mallarméan equation, and which rests on the Platonic concept that music is the supreme wisdom. Music as an ecstasy is a development of the Platonic idea of the purgative value of music which, according to Plato, was given by God (*Laws*, II, 653D). Music was therefore the Idea—source of all, the soul of the universe; the Pythagorean numbers were nothing else but the means to reach the Idea—the heavenly music of Plato. Such a music could not be heard through the senses, and the supreme wisdom of Plato lay in silence. There is no distance between the supreme wisdom of Plato, situated beyond the perceptual world, and the mystic union of God's lover with God; both take place in silence and timelessness. The Socratean and neo-Platonic way through negation as being the way to knowledge and experience of "the One" or Supreme wisdom, is also the way of the Christian mystics. It is the way of the English mystic who wrote *The Cloud of Unknowing*, in which it is stated that the soul in this life is always between two clouds, a cloud of forgetting beneath, which hides all creatures, and a cloud of unknowing above, upon which it must smite with a sharp dart of longing love. The same method is advocated by St. John of the Cross in *The Ascent of Mount Carmel*:

In order to arrive at having pleasure in everything
Desire to have pleasure in nothing.
In order to arrive at possessing everything
Desire to possess nothing.

Descartes' method of negation in order to reach an intuitive awareness of existence, is also a method of arriving at the positive through successive negations. Pascal's scepticism rests on the same principle; it is different from that of Montaigne, which is purely intellectual—scepticism for scepticism's sake—and therefore is, in its way, a kind of fideism; so, in the end, is Nietzsche's negation of Christianity and replacement by anthropomorphism and will, and so is Sartre's belief in Freedom for Freedom's sake.

In the end, the Idea, source of the Platonic universe, is music, the music of the highest sphere, the ninth sphere in Dante, but not the music of the planets and even less human music which, as Mallarmé and Poe say, is sound without ideas. The music which Mallarmé is trying to reach is the Idea which contains both music and the word. Pythagoras, and later Galileo, thought the Idea could be reached through mathematical signs or symbols, and Vico held a similar belief when he said:

There must necessarily exist, as part of the very nature of created things, a common, essential language capable of universally describing the substance of things. If the erudites would consent to direct their researches towards such an aim, they could compute an essential vocabulary common to all language.[1]

That was obviously the aim of Rimbaud and of Mallarmé, who says:

Je me figure par un indéracinable sans doute préjugé d'écrivain, que rien ne demeurera sans être proféré; que

[1] G. B. Vico, *Scienza Nuova Seconda* (1744), Libro I (Sezione II), xxii, 161.

nous en sommes là, précisément, à rechercher, devant une brisure des grands rythmes littéraires (il en a été question plus haut) et leur éparpillement en frissons articulés proches de l'instrumentation, un art d'achever la transposition, au Livre, de la symphonie ou uniment de reprendre notre bien: car, ce n'est pas de sonorités élémentaires par les cuivres, les cordes, les bois, indéniablement mais de l'intellectuelle parole à son apogée que doit avec plénitude et évidence, résulter, en tant que l'ensemble des rapports existant dans tout, la Musique.[1]

That dream of Mallarmé to enclose all in a book was also that of Joyce, who tried to realise it in *Finnegan's Wake*. Both Mallarmé and Joyce are the direct descendants of Flaubert, who says in his *Correspondance* that he dreamt of writing a book which would be nothing else but a book, a book which would only live by the strength of his style. The Mallarmé, who wrote in *Un Coup de Dés*:

RIEN

N'AURA EU LIEU

QUE LE LIEU

EXCEPTÉ

PEUT-ÊTRE

UNE CONSTELLATION

is related to Flaubert and Villiers de L'Isle-Adam on one side, and on the other to Joyce and Proust—both searchers of the absolute; all believers in the idea that life exists not to be lived but to be expressed: "As for living, our servants will do that for us", had said Villiers de L'Isle-Adam. For Mallarmé,

[1] Op. cit., pp. 367–8.

everything exists to be transposed into a book, and the trans-position takes place musically; music is not the end but the means to reach the Idea:

> Je pose, à mes risques esthétiquement, cette conclusion (si, par quelque grâce, absente, toujours, d'un exposé, je vous amenai à la ratifier, ce serait l'honneur pour moi cherché ce soir): que la Musique et les Lettres sont la face alternative ici élargie vers l'obscur; scintillante là, avec certitude, d'un phénomène, le seul, je l'appelai, l'Idée.[1]

For Mallarmé there cannot be any æsthetic pleasure without the Idea. Music and letters are various ways of expressing the Idea, and the one which holds pre-eminence over the other is the one in which the Idea comes out more clearly than in the other which, in fact, only lends to the first all its attributes, in order to help it to bring out the Idea.

Mallarmé would have liked to invent a form of speech which would have had enough musical qualities to compete with other forms of music purely based on sound. That was the aim of his poetry, the aim to bring back music and letters to the original unity, and therefore we can understand why, when Debussy proposed to put *L'Après-midi d'un Faune* to music, Mallarmé serenely said: "But I thought I had already done it." One man had, in some ways, succeeded in doing what Mallarmé wanted to do—Richard Wagner; and Mallarmé admired him not for the revolution he brought about in instrumentation and composition, but for having fused into unity word and sound. Mallarmé, like most poets, understood music in his own way, which was not the orthodox way of musicians; his daughter says about him that: "jeune il la dédaignait",[2] and Noulet says: "Quand Mallarmé commença à suivre les concerts Lamoureux en 1885, il était déjà prisonnier de sa légende et veillait à ressembler au personnage qu'on veut

[1] Mallarmé, op. cit., p. 649.
[2] Geneviève Bonniot-Mallarmé, 'Mallarmé par sa fille', *Nouvelle Revue Française*, 1 November 1926.

qu'il soit."[1] In *Richard Wagner, Rêverie d'un poète français,*
"Mallarmé does not praise the poet for being a musician but
for having invented the total poem, word and music, thought
and rhythm, the poem which is idea, décor, dance and song,
divine unity."[2] Mallarmé had the same aim: "Singulier défi
qu'aux poètes dont il usurpe le devoir avec la plus candide et
splendide bravoure, inflige Richard Wagner!"[3]

In the poem *Hommage,* Mallarmé makes it clear that Wagner
was in music the god which in poetry he, Mallarmé, was not.
But the differences between Mallarmé and Wagner were
profound. Mallarmé and Wagner were at one in their attempts
to fuse into a whole poetry and music. Yet Beethoven had
already done that in the Ninth Symphony, and he had done it
in the way in which Mallarmé wanted to do it, and which is
by moving from music to the words and not, as Wagner had
proceeded, from words to music in order to express a depth
of emotion which words could not express. But in the end
Mallarmé neither gives pre-eminence to music, nor does he
move towards the words; he moves musically towards the
idea, source of music and word; his journey is neither that of
Beethoven nor that of Wagner. Mallarmé was concerned with
a poetry of suggestiveness and fleeting hints, while Wagner's
music is very literary, together with characters which are
powerfully stressed and with a definite coherence. The conception of music which is also that of Mallarmé is Debussy's—
the open reaction to Wagner. With him we have the melodic
fragmentation and the lack of definite harmonic lines, together
with impressionistic fireworks and stress on sound and colour,
rather than on the rigid construction of the notes. In glorifying
Wagner, Mallarmé still thinks of his dream of inventing a form
of speech which would contain, and also protect, the poetic
mystery. Music was a source of analogy, but he was firmly
convinced that poetry alone had the means to express the

[1] Op. cit., p. 269.   [2] Ibid.
[3] Mallarmé, op. cit., p. 541.

ineffable, the very essence of things. He insists that: "La Poésie, proche l'idée, est Musique, par excellence—ne consent pas d'infériorité."[1] Or: "Je sais qu'on veut à la musique limiter le mystère quand l'écrit y prétend."[2] Or again: "A quelle hauteur qu'exultent les cordes et les cuivres, un vers, du fait de l'approche immédiate de l'âme, y atteint."[3] The point is clear enough: Mallarmé saw in music a source of analogies, a means to an end, but not an end in itself. "Observe", he says, "how the instruments detach, with a spell easy to grasp, the summit of natural landscapes, vaporise and anew combine them, floating in a higher state. See how, to express the forest, merged in twilight green horizon, there needs only such strains, where the hunt is barely remembered; or the meadow, whose waning afternoon's pastoral fluidity is now reflected and dispelled in river echoes. A line, a few brief vibrations, the suggestion is complete."[4] Here is the true lesson which music offers to the poet—a line, a brief vibration to represent a forest or a river—fluidity and freedom from the static imagery of the Parnassians. "Parler n'a trait à la réalité des choses que commercialement: en littérature, cela se contente d'y faire une allusion ou de distraire leur qualité qu'incorporera quelque idée."[5]

Schopenhauer had been the first to see in music the supreme

---

[1] Ibid., p. 381.   [2] Ibid., p. 385.   [3] Ibid., p. 389.
[4] Ibid., p. 522. Besides that, there is the importance of silence as part of the structure of music; there we have intervals, pauses, quavers and semi-quavers carefully regulated as part of the harmony. Why should not silence play the same part in the structure of poetry? Maeterlinck thought so; so did Claudel when he said: "Le poème . . . est fait du blanc qui reste sur le papier". Mallarmé had anticipated them all, and in the most systematic way, in *Un Coup de Dés*. Valéry, reflecting on that poem (*Variété II*, 'Le coup de Dés') found that the white of the page or the spatial importance of silence as a means to determine the field of the words (something strangely reminiscent of Einstein's theory of the importance of spatial fields) had played a capital part in the poem: "il me sembla de voir la figure d'une pensée, pour la première fois placée dans notre espace. . . . Ici véritablement l'étendue parlait, songeait, enfantait des formes temporelles. L'attente, le doute, la concentration étaient choses visibles. Ma vue avait affaire à des silences qui auraient pris corps. . . . Là sur le papier même . . . coexistait la Parole!"
[5] Ibid., p. 366.

art; the world, according to him, could be an objectification of the will as well as an incarnation of music, which is the supreme will—the soul of the universe. By saying "that music expresses the metaphysical aspect of the physical world, the essence of every phenomenon", he renews the Platonist concept of music. Nietzsche also says: "Music expresses the divine becoming which informs things and life."

Schiller had shown, before Mallarmé, preoccupations which are not different from his: "When I sit down to write a poem, what I most often see in front of me is the musical aspect of the poem and not a clear concept of the subject, which sometimes is not quite clear in my mind."

The analogy between poetry and music has been fully grasped by modern poets from Mallarmé onwards. They have more and more freed themselves from the dependence of the story in the long poem. Poe had suggested that development in his disquisition on *The Raven*, which is nevertheless a story in verse. Already in *L'Après-midi d'un Faune* the story is vague and unimportant, and when we come to the major poems of our time, like *La Jeune Parque*, *The Waste Land* or *Four Quartets*, there is no story; it is replaced by musical themes holding together fluctuating psychological states; and the analogy with music has come closest in *Four Quartets*, which, with their themes, counter-themes, figures and revolutions developed in various phrases and keys, have the structure of a musical composition. The attitude of Mallarmé towards music can best be understood by reading his article called 'L'Art pour tous', which he published in *L'Artiste* on 15 September 1862: from that date to the time when he wrote 'Le Mystère dans les Lettres', his ideas about poetry did not change.

Toute chose sacrée et qui veut demeurer sacrée s'enveloppe de mystère. Les religions se retranchent à l'abri d'arcanes dévoilés au seul prédestiné: l'art a les siens. . . .

J'ai souvent demandé pourquoi ce caractère nécessaire a

été refusé à un seul art, au plus grand. Celui-là est sans mystère contre les curiosités hypocrites, sans terreur contre les impiétés, ou sous le sourire et la grimace de l'ignorant et de l'ennemi.

Je parle de la poésie. . . .

Ainsi les premiers venus entrent de plain-pied dans un chef-d'œuvre et depuis qu'il y a des poètes, il n'a pas été inventé, pour l'écartement de ces importuns, une langue immaculée, . . . et ces intrus tiennent en façon de carte d'entrée une page de l'alphabet où ils ont appris à lire ![1]

This article is of capital importance, for it explains Mallarmé's attitude to music and poetry and the causes of his hermetism, something which is against the genius of the French language. Mallarmé did not cultivate obscurity for obscurity's sake, he wanted to "vaincre le hasard mot par mot . . . et authentiquer le silence",[2] and he wanted to render poetry inaccessible to the non-initiated and to those who were not prepared to make the necessary effort to penetrate the mystery.

Art was for him, as for Flaubert, something sacred, and he did not wish to have it profaned.

POETRY AND TRANSCENDENCE

Mallarmé believed in the mystery of poetry, for him the means to reveal through art the world which only existed for that revelation, and he believed that poetry had to be protected from vulgar curiosity. Both points of view are closely related and converge towards the single conclusion of art as a sacred ritual expressed in words which have become the means to abolish the real and to transform it into the ideal. The words, purified from everyday usage, have regained their original power of music and speech and can reveal in each case the idea, part of the supreme Idea (akin to Plato's), to be contained in

---

[1] Mallarmé, op. cit., 'L'Art pour tous', pp. 257-8.
[2] Mallarmé, p. 387.

the great book which would reveal the world. In a way this is similar to certain mathematicians' attempts to reduce the representation of the universe to an equation or a mathematical formula; in fact it is the search of Einstein, it is the 'cosmical number' of Eddington. We are here close to the demiurgic belief of Rimbaud, a belief which restores to the word the creative force of the 'logos'.

Valéry, repeating Rousseau, had said: "Il n'est rien de si beau que ce qui n'existe pas", yet Shakespeare and Keats had already suggested this form of truth:

> There's not the smallest orb which thou behold'st
> But in his motion like an angel sings,
> Still quiring to the young-eyed cherubins;
> Such harmony is in immortal souls;
> But whilst this muddy vesture of decay
> Doth grossly close it in, we cannot hear it.
>
> <div align="right">(<i>Merchant of Venice</i>, v, 1)</div>

> Heard melodies are sweet, but those unheard
> Are sweeter; therefore, ye soft pipes play on;
> Not to the sensual ear, but, more endear'd,
> Pipe to the spirit ditties of no tone.
>
> <div align="right">(<i>Ode to a Grecian Urn</i>)[1]</div>

that sets the Platonic theme that intellectual or celestial music is eternal, for heard melodies are merely fleeting. Mallarmé, who could have subscribed to Plato's aphorism, repeated by Pater, that "all art aspires to music", rediscovers for himself the Platonic and Pythagorean conception that the universe is musically constructed, and that the human soul, which is similarly formed, cannot hear through the sensorial apparatus of the body the celestial music of its source. Therefore heard music is inferior to unheard music which is the true wisdom

---

[1] Cf. W. B. Yeats, who, longing to escape "the fury and the mire of human veins" wishes to be gathered "unto the artifice of eternity".
(Bysantium, and Sailing to Bysantium)

of Plato, who seems to have thrown forth so many of the fundamental images which form our thought.

For Mallarmé, language was a means to free the real, the true cosmic vision. Like Blake, he did not believe in sensorial reality; the divergence between Mallarmé and Blake is twofold. First, the extraordinary faculty which transcends the real and grasps the ideal world is not the same. For Blake, it is imagination, the faculty which through metaphors and images can give life to the invisible. For Mallarmé, it is more a kind of abstracting and 'neantising'[1] power, which does not aim at creating any concrete æsthetic experience but, on the contrary, at creating the evanescence of an experience, or what one may describe as an experience 'neantised', emptied of itself, for, in the end, the aim of Mallarmé is to reach nothingness, source of all things: "Je profère la parole pour la replonger dans son inanité." The processes employed in both cases are different: Blake believed in revelations and visions of an eternal world, and he believed in the existence of a transcendental reality; Mallarmé does not believe in a transcendental world, but he believes in transcendence—transcendence of the word as 'logos', therefore transcendence of the æsthetic experience, and since, although not a transcendentalist, he believed in transcendence (the difference between the two is very slim), his road to transcendence took place along Cartesian lines of willed conscious effort. Blake ignored realities; for him, a true Platonist, they were only the reflections of the ideal world which was the true world. Mallarmé, Descartes, and also Valéry negate reality by an act of will—they wilfully pretend to believe that nothing exists except their thoughts, and from that wilful 'neantisation' of reality surges the intuitive awareness of their existence, the positive assertion of their thought which, after a series of negations, reaches the point when there

---

[1] I use the neologism, 'neantise' (French *néantiser*—to turn into nothingness) because the English word 'annihilate' does not seem to carry to the full that meaning. The abstracting power could be the intellect of Plato.

is nothing more to negate except negation itself, which is also the negation of time—*le hasard* of Mallarmé—and the means to reach the pure essential self. Mallarmé proceeds along lines similar to those of Descartes and, up to a certain point, quite concordant with those of Descartes. He too passes from negation to assertion through will which becomes in both cases the foundation of their epistemological methods, and in the end it is in either case a problem of knowledge, of consciousness of existence and not a metaphysical proof of existence; indeed, doubt and 'neantisation' can only be philosophical attitudes based on existence, for existentially they are self-contradictory, they would imply the destruction of being. Doubt cannot prove existence since it presupposes it, it can only prove the consciousness of existence; existence itself is, and is beyond proof, its only possible ontological proof is death, and a death which could only be apprehended as such within the context of eternity.

The fundamental divergence between Mallarmé and Descartes, the divergence which brings Mallarmé nearer to Hegel[1] than to Descartes, is that Descartes implicitly posits God as the prime mover of Creation while Mallarmé does not, implicitly or explicitly; the result is that Descartes starts from a methodological progressive doubt towards nothingness which, of course, since there is somewhere a God, can never be absolute. Mallarmé sets himself in the place of God, he does not proceed methodologically, he 'neantises' the material world absolutely, as a whole, and posits its non-existence in order to assert the existence of something which, he knows, is not, yet which is going to be in his own mind, and, by so doing, he of course asserts his own existence. Mallarmé attempts a metaphysical act, Descartes does not, he only says: "I think, therefore I am" but Mallarmé says: "I create, therefore I am", an equation

[1] The great principle of thesis, anti-thesis and synthesis corresponds to being, non-being and existence. The essence of being is to keep non-being virtual, therefore part of existence, so that the anti-thesis, although necessary, can never become the thesis.

which could be replaced by the word 'God'. For Mallarmé, as well as for God, creation—the word—is the *logos*, and Mallarmé dreamt all his life of discovering that *logos* which would embody the whole of creation. He believed that by refusing to believe in the existence of all things which were not his Dream, he could give life to his Dream which was literature:

> Je réponds par une exagération, certes, et vous en prévenant.—Oui, que la Littérature existe, *et si l'on veut, seule, à l'exclusion de tout.*[1]

Then he goes on to say that one can perfectly deny what is, in order to assert the existence of what is not, knowing full well that this is a lie.

> Je vénère comment, par une supercherie, on projette, à quelque élévation défendue et de foudre! le conscient manque chez nous de ce qui là-haut éclate.[2]

> Je *veux*, [he wrote in 1866] je veux me donner ce spectacle de la matière, ayant conscience d'être, et, cependant, s'élançant forcément dans ce Rêve qu'elle *sait n'être pas* . . . et proclamant devant le Rien qui est la Vérité, ces glorieux mensonges.[3]

But that operation takes place amidst suffering and great risks of complete frustration and sterility, for everything rests on the possible flight of the poet who has no air (the real) to beat his wings against in order to rise and who, therefore, is condemned to failure. In his god-like attempts to create out of nothingness, the poet must first destroy or rather 'neantise' all.

> Luxe, ô salle d'ébène où, pour séduire un roi
> Se tordent dans leur mort des guirlandes célèbres . . .
> Vous n'êtes qu'un orgueil menti par les ténèbres
> Aux yeux du solitaire ébloui de sa foi.[4]

[1] Mallarmé, op. cit., p. 646.   [2] Ibid., p. 647.
[3] Quoted by Mondor, op. cit., p. 193.
[4] *Quand l'ombre menaça*, Mallarmé, op. cit., p. 67.

Everything has been annihilated so that the flame may rise which the poet knows to be unreal. Yet one must note one vital point, and it is this—that even in Mallarmé, nothingness is not absolute, for he says:

> Oui, je sais qu'au lointain de cette nuit, la Terre
> Jette d'un grand éclat l'insolite mystère
> Sous les siècles hideux qui l'obscurcissent moins.[1]

This contradicts "la peur des espaces infinis" of Pascal; it means that the human spirit cannot be crushed by the universe which is nothing compared with the light and splendour of the human mind. Mallarmé was an atheist, but he had faith in the spirit, and what is the spirit but the breath of God? This poem ends with a message of optimism and supreme courage which we do not find anywhere else in Mallarmé's poetry; not only can the creative act save the universe from nothingness, but, instead of the frozen paralysis which is the conclusion of *Le Cygne* and other poems, we see here that the creative act is accepted as possible. The earth and matter are no longer, but they continue to have, somehow, a kind of ideal existence. They have become the very image of creation in the mind of the one who has abolished it and replaced it by his Dream, by his vision:

> L'espace à soi pareil qu'il accroisse ou se nie
> Roule dans cet ennui des feux vils pour témoins
> Que s'est d'un astre en fête allumé le génie.[2]

The position has been reversed, the real has now nearly vanished and only remains as a proof of the existence of thought which has replaced it. The only constellations are not "les étoiles feux vils", but those which live in the mind of the poet in a space which never changes and where "une attirance supérieure . . . détache les choses jusqu'à s'en remplir et

[1] Op. cit., p. 67. [2] Ibid.

aussi les douer de resplendissements à travers l'espace vacant, en des fêtes à volonté et solitaires".[1]

Words have become the real, things and matter the evanescence. Mallarmé's creation, analogous to divine creation, does not start from the same premise of absolute nothingness containing both being and non-being, it starts from a creation which has been 'neantised', but which has left traces of its existence in the words;[2] it has been essentialised and replaced by words which are as free as possible from the contingent; it is entirely based on the poetic act which surges from this willed nothingness, embraces past and future and is the only existential proof that silence truly is. In the case of Mallarmé as in the case of Valéry, it seems to be evident that the fact that they wrote implies a belief in the transcendence of the creative act—Valéry's scepticism, Mallarmé's philosophical suicide being merely a method in order to reach a transcendence which, in the end, confers to poetic duration an ontological value.

Neither Mallarmé nor even less Valéry could be described as Platonists in the accepted meaning of the word, implying the existence of an ideal world whose reflection is the real; yet, if one tries to track down the exact meaning given to the *logos*, born from, and testimony of silence, one cannot fail to realise that at the end of its ascending movement, the *logos* of Mallarmé, shorn as much as possible of contingent stains, meets the Idea of Plato. What Mallarmé does is not to posit the ideal world and, with it, a belief in revelation, but to posit the possibility of reaching through mental processes, based on words, and terminating in words, the flash of experience which reveals eternity. One could say that eternity could only be revealed, or mentally discovered, because it is, for somehow,

[1] Mallarmé, op. cit., p. 647.
[2] In the poem *Sainte* typical of the Mallarméan journey, the conventional perceptual image of the beginning is abolished and fades into the twilight to become a wing, and finally the image of a harp upon which plays the "musicienne du silence".

whatever the mental operations and the processes followed by Mallarmé, Descartes, Valéry or Blake or anybody else, one realises that one can only deal with things which already are and which, although they can offer to sense-observation and to revelations in time, various facets, are in their essence timeless. Even more, the urge for the search, for the discovery, is in itself the very proof of the reality that there is something to search for; Mallarmé's aim was "de tout confondre dans un poétique baiser",[1] to give an orphic explanation of creation; for that he had to separate "comme en vue d'attributions différentes le double état de la parole, brut ou immédiat ici, là essentiel",[2] in order to "donner un sens plus pur aux mots de la tribu".[3] He attempted to find in human language the essence of language, and he came to realise that the *logos*—God's expression—was beyond the human, and could not be heard or apprehended, for it was silence—the absolute, source of all things—and the poet, if he were absolutely logical, could only remain silent. Both Valéry and Mallarmé tried it, yet in the end they both resumed their attempts to reach silence—attempts which form the most fundamental problem of literature.

For Mallarmé, involved, as he says, in the attempt "d'instituer un jeu, on ne sait, qui confirme la fiction",[4] the words are signs, musical or mathematical signs standing for something else and employed in order to discover the great unknown. In Mallarmé, language has two functions: reporting facts and transposing facts into 'ideas', which is creation.

Je dis: une fleur, et hors de l'oubli où ma voix relègue aucun contour, en tant que quelque chose d'autre que les calices sus, musicalement se lève, idée même et sauve, l'absente de tous bouquets.[5]

[1] Mallarmé, op. cit., p. 264.
[2] Ibid., p. 368.
[3] Ibid., p. 189.
[4] Ibid., p. 380.
[5] Ibid., p. 368.

The 'absent from all bouquets' is the flower which is beyond the perceptual world; the real has been abolished and what we have left is the 'idea' of flower which can be any flower. There are here no limits set to the imagination. The word 'musicalement' indicates that in the abstracting process, the ideas combine like musical notes and harmonies, and tend toward the harmony of Platonic Ideas. Reality has been evaporated, transformed into its essence in a process similar to music in which the musical instruments represent reality in their own way. We are here at the core of Mallarmé's attitude towards music and what he meant by music as vague art. Music is, on the contrary, as far as composition is concerned, an art of mathematical precision. There is no vagueness in the quantitative value of the notes, they have the value of mathematical or algebraic signs, but, like mathematical signs, they stand for something else, for affective and mental values. Therefore, the musical notes arrayed or played according to the laws of rhythm are each the starting points of affective and intellectual ripples which follow the graph of the rhythm; they are like lights being turned on one after the other, and each one illuminating its peculiar area of darkness, yet the geometric line which links them up is the line of the road, just as the ideal line which links the words is the metre of the poem.

In Mallarmé's poetry, each word anticipates and merges into the next, therefore only exists in its dual capacity of projection backward and forward axled on a state of virtuality which is the continuous becoming of the word. Each word becomes alight, burns and transmits the fire, just as a flame runs along an igniting cord, dragging with it its load of past, and so on, until in this mounting process of past and projection forward, we reach the end of the poem, with all the creative force of the words having accumulated and ready to fade away finally in the white heat of the page; and the process can be repeated as often as the reader is capable of living through its duration. In Mallarmé the words are used as much as possible like musical notes or signs; they have been deprived by various syntactical distortions of their logical meaning so that they never produce a static picture in the Parnassian style; their aim is to give life by continuity and movement, a movement which, like dance, lives and dies at the meeting-point of the music and the dancer's gesture which embodies it. The poem only lives in the flash of apprehension. It is music both in its means and effects, and in its essence, and it is an evanescent flight reaching towards perfection in as far as it eliminates the contingent and approaches silence. Mallarmé believed that the poet's task was to reabsorb the contingent by thought and word into the absolute, and so to do away with *le hasard*—creation, the flaw in the perfect diamond of non-being. This is, of course, an operation which not only presupposes an absolute, or God—source of creation—but also a concept of God which is expressed in the poet's act, trying to destroy creation in order to recreate the absolute. This the poet tries to do by seeing the essence of things, by eliminating the contingent from things, and by expressing those essences in symbols. By so doing he vanquishes time: "Le travail d'un artiste", says Valéry in *Eupalinos*, "quand il fait immédiatement et par sa volonté suivie un tel buste [celui d'Apollon], n'est-il pas, en quelque sorte, le contraire du temps indéfini?"[1] Language is used both symbolically and also musically as a kind of magic aiming at creating a state of trance whence will rise the unheard music, the vision of the absolute. We have here an ideal of pure poetry which entails the most highly conscious technique, a real science of words used as symbols.[2] Yet such an ideal is condemned to failure, for the words, part of creation, can never be rid completely of the contingent, and therefore they cannot destroy *le hasard*—creation. Mallarmé recognised that, and in *Un Coup de Dés jamais n'abolira le Hasard* accepted the fact that

[1] P. Valéry, *Eupalinos* (Gallimard, Paris, 1944), p. 80.
[2] The poet is a kind of pure mathematician; Valéry, Mallarmé's disciple, loved mathematics and was apparently, according to Gide, extremely proficient in them.

poetry could only be absolute silence and that his art was, in the end, *une impasse.*

There is, of course, plenty of music in the normally accepted meaning of the word in Mallarmé's poems—we have sounds echoing one another, we have rhymes and assonances, and we have subtle sinuous rhythms imitating actions. One has only to think of the harmonies in 'i' as in the sonnet *Le vierge, le vivace, et le bel aujourd'hui,* to realise what Mallarmé could do with the orchestration of one single vowel. But the kind of musical effect he was after was above all that which did away with the individuality of the words and enabled him to use them in a poem not as entities with a life of their own but in the same way as musical notes integrated in a musical composition. Just as dance surges from the void of the stage, in the same way his poems surge from the emptiness of the page and create an illusion which is dispelled once the dancers have left the stage or when one has come, in the end, to the blank of the page. The words and the dance create their space, just as movement creates its duration; thence the importance of the page which is for Mallarmé the absence whence the illusion which transcends it in the creative moment is going to rise. We have moved away from the ideal of plastic art realised statically towards an art of movement realised in continuity;[1] most of Mallarmé's images are images of evanescence, which merely rise to suggest and to fade away. Rhythm is more primal than words, products of reason, and is more intimately connected with the organic life of the body. Poetry is, as it has often been said, the expression of human emotion. The words describe it intellectually but do not live it, except in so far as the rhythm which emerges from them reproduces or conveys the original rhythm which was at the source of the emotion. The words depicting it are the termini of the original rhythm which has given them birth; therefore, starting from them, one could

[1] By now this is true for painting, sculpture and music as well as for literature.

imaginatively recover that rhythm and the original emotion itself, if one is in front of a genuine and successfully expressed poetic experience.

For Mallarmé, poetic creation is essentially the transcendence through art of nothingness and negation. His poems are on the whole the 'existential' fiction of something that the poet knows to be unreal, something which he creates wilfully in order to abolish *le hasard*. The Mallarméan poem is a duration, a projection out of time through thought, creating its own space and laws, imitations of temporal and spacial laws. It is the creation of a moment both transient, since it is based on thought, and perennial, since it is free from the contingent and is as close as possible to the original intuitive apprehension of the world by the God-like act, and it is, in the end, the self projected in the absolute and transformed "tel qu'en lui-même enfin l'éternité le change". Each poem is a new philosophical suicide of the poet's self, and therefore an abolition of time in order to reach the transcendental self, a kind of phœnix-like operation to rise from nowhere to nowhere. The poetic vision surges from and transcends nothingness in the duration of the poem, but neither the poem nor the spacial duration where the poem is situated acquires a positive value; they lie beyond nothingness, as the negation of that nothingness, a fiction, a wilful acceptance of what is not. Thence despair and frustration born from the awareness that the poet-Atlas holding eternity may at any moment lose his grip on nothingness, source of his positiveness, and fall through eternity. As the poet's existence is based on the negation of a negation, he cannot but fear that at any moment the negating mind based on nothingness might negate itself and fall into absolute nothingness. The poet is the transcendental will without any origin or end to sustain him; he has usurped God's main attribute. We are at the very essence of subjectivity as pure will in action, the will of Schopenhauer: "The world as will". Here the will is and is not, and in fact it can only be, if it knows that it can also not be, therefore at any moment one can pass from a positive to a negative state, one is at the mercy of *le hasard*—which is creation—a terrifying alternative which can only be transformed into the security of no fear of alternatives by the abolition of creation and a return to non-being and silence. Mallarmé accepted the risk and tried to abolish *le hasard*, and Valéry dared to live on the verge of the void. But those who came after them did not show the same extreme courage, and many sought refuge in non-consciousness or in nihilism.

CHAPTER VII

Conclusion

FRENCH romanticism is not so very different from French classicism. The fundamental difference lies in the themes, the situations, and in the intrusion of the author who now describes the reality which is in himself and not external reality; he no longer says: "I think, therefore I am", but: "I feel, therefore I am"; yet he still bases the proof of existence on the cognitive act, which this time rests on the affective rather than intellectual aspect of human life. The underlying belief of the romantic age seems to be that subjective reality described objectively is the reality of all; it is in some ways a form of Hegelianism with its interpolarity of rational and real, but with rational replaced by sensorial; in some ways only, for the fundamental aspect of Hegelianism, that is the impossibility to individuate and the stress on the necessary universality of knowledge are lacking and will not fully emerge until the second half of the nineteenth century, after a brief phase of scientific realism which seems to be the final shedding off of that amount of Cartesianism which had gone into the universalism of Hegel. In spite of the Kantian belief in the 'noumenon', the belief in mystery, together with the idea that true knowledge is both subjective and universal in the fact that it requires both an organic oneness of the subject-object relationship and integration into the whole, is very slow to emerge in France.

French romantics only took the husk of things, while they remained unaware of the core. They were so consciously set on the necessity of being different from their fathers and forefathers, that they forgot the elementary truth that either one is different from others, and therefore one does not consciously think of oneself as different, or one thinks oneself different and then one is merely thinking and nothing more. That is in the end the real problem of 'originality' in art. A true poet cannot but be, in some ways, different from his predecessors and contemporaries, but he knows that he would cease to be different as soon as he consciously tried to be so. That seems to be the case with French romantics and with Victor Hugo in particular. There were, at that time, great talks of revolutionary changes, yet no profound changes took place in poetry. The rhetoric of Victor Hugo is of another order from that of Corneille, but not of another quality; it is still rhetoric; it is more emotional, more colourful, more laden with sense-data, but it still is as dialectical; it aims at convincing the heart rather than the mind, I agree, but conviction was nevertheless the aim. Though there is a big difference between the means used, as far as ends are concerned, Victor Hugo's are not very different from Voltaire's. Both were, in various degrees, much concerned with expressing their 'philosophies'; Voltaire's cerebralism is certainly very different from Hugo's emotional rhetoric, yet in both cases it is rhetoric, which, of course, in the case of the latter, can rise often enough to great poetry.

French romantics, the theorists of the movement in particular, entertained the rather naïve idea that if they stripped verse of all the rags and tatters which were now covering it, they would automatically find poetry. They failed to realise that poetry had long since died, that they were only dealing with rags and tatters with nothing under them, for the whole of the eighteenth century had been quite content to produce glittering dresses worn by mechanical models, unaware of the fact that the dress is nothing without the shape of flesh and blood which ripples under it, and that there is more beauty in a hand or in the transparent skin of a Rembrandt than in all the shadowy drapery and tinsel of neo-classical art. Voltaire had

149

strutted about in Racine's mantle, Victor Hugo thought that
by pulling the mantle off his shoulders he would find, under it,
Racine; he only found Voltaire; he thought that by making his
children romp or sing in Shakespearian rags, Shakespeare
would leave Stratford-on-Avon and come to Paris or to
Jersey; that did not happen, so we only had Victor Hugo,
something to be proud of, but something very remote from
Shakespeare. In most things the French romantics only caught
the echoes and not the real voice; in their haste to be original
by escaping from the rules and conventions of the seventeenth
century, they failed to detect under these conventions the true
poignancy which links Racine to Villon, and they remained
irremediably themselves, wearing masks and saying repeatedly
that they were what they would have liked to be, when
everybody, including themselves, knew in truth that they only
were what they were.

What can one say about the great poetic revolution so much
talked about by Lamartine in his 1849 preface to his *Méditations
Poétiques*, or by Victor Hugo in *Réponse à un acte d'accusation*:

> Je fis souffler un vent révolutionnaire,
> Je mis un bonnet rouge au vieux dictionnaire?

—mere words. The old alexandrine still remained, and, in
some ways, the worse for wear when compared with the
beauty which it had in the hands of Racine. How could there
be 'a revolution' since there was hardly any change in sensibility? It is true that feelings and emotions had returned to the
poetic stage; French romantic poets felt strongly; and in truth,
the capacity to feel is the measure of one's capacity to transcend
existence; but feelings are only the raw materials which imagination must transmute into poetry; and there lies the flaw.
Strange as it may seem, true imagination, not fancy, plays no
outstanding part in French romanticism; feelings and emotions
are expounded and arrayed according to the best laws of
rhetoric, but, on the whole, they are not lived through

imaginatively; they do not become part of an experience which transforms existence into life, they merely suffuse that experience rendered in perfect linguistic constructions with hardly any metaphysical resonances. Of course, one must not go too far on these lines; there is the Victor Hugo of his later years, the Victor Hugo of *La Trompette du Jugement*, *Dieu*, *La Fin de Satan*, etc., but how inchoate some of his pseudo-philosophical flights and how traditional and perfectly rhetorical some of his lyrical poems, even the best—those like *A Villequier* or *Tristesse d'Olympio*! How different from the lyricism of Shelley—the Shelley of *The Triumph of Life* and *The Sensitive Plant*—or from Keats' odes, how composed they can sound when compared with *Kubla Khan* or with the magnificent songs of Blake! We really had to wait for Nerval, Baudelaire, Rimbaud and Verlaine with his words: "Prends l'éloquence et tords-lui son cou", to see lyrical poetry free itself from rhetoric and return to the intensity, the apparent naturalness of the poetry of Villon, or the sense of mystery which it had with the English romantics. What French romantic poetry lacks is the quality which, as early as 1829, Sainte-Beuve would have liked to find in all poetry—the capacity of: "Faire saillir un je ne sais quoi par une idéalisation admirable".[1] No French romantic poet, with the exception of the later Hugo, until Rimbaud and Nerval, shows the visionary imagination and the sense of mystery of Blake, Coleridge, Shelley or Hölderlin. It is only with the Victor Hugo of the exile, the Hugo of *La Légende des Siècles*, *La Fin de Satan* and *Les Quatre Vents de l'Esprit* that visions, mystery, ghosts and apocalyptic utterances find their place in French poetry. That was the Victor Hugo about whom Rimbaud, in his letter of 15 May 1871, said "qu'il avait été *voyant*". That was the Victor Hugo who had said "It is within oneself that one must look for what is without. The dark mirror is deep down in man. There is the terrible chiaroscuro. A thing reflected in the mind is more

---

[1] *Pensées de Joseph Delorme*, XVI, p. 155.

vertiginous than seen directly. It is more than an image—it is a simulacrum, and in the simulacrum there is a spectre . . . when we lean over this well, we see there, at an abysmal depth in a narrow circle, the great world itself."[1] But even the magnificent later poetry of Hugo is never completely free from declamation and diffuseness.

The belief underlying French romanticism still is that the phenomenal and supra-phenomenal world can be apprehended and depicted through art. The artist, convinced that he expresses all aspects of reality, subjectively of course, distorts them by limiting them, and by imposing upon them his own limitations. The awareness that being, in time, cannot, can never describe, through its contingent means, the reality of eternity which is part of existence, is lacking. The cosmic visions of Victor Hugo, one of the most powerful visual imaginations ever at work in literature, convey a feeling of vastness and universality, but, on the whole, not of complete mystery. The reason behind that seems to me that they are not an emergence of the mystery through a subjectivity which, as such, would be equal to no subjectivity, but the projection of a subjectivity on what is thought to be the mystery. It is not therefore the phenomenon, reflection of the 'noumenon', apprehended subjectively in moments in which the subject ceases to be subject and becomes the spiritual experience lived, it is rather a permeation of the phenomenal and supra-phenomenal world by the subject which seeks to master the whole. The result is wilfulness, and not submission and acceptance; we have intellectual interference in processes which are beyond the intellect; yet this seems unavoidable, for visual imagination tends to impose upon things and feelings a precision and conceptualisation which they cannot have. When that type of imagination is applied to poetry, we have, not a climate or atmosphere resting on sensuous representation where the

[1] Victor Hugo, *Contemplations Suprêmes, Post-scriptum de ma vie*, pp. 236–7 (translation by H. Read).

mystery remains, ready to be born different, yet in certain ways similar, for each reader, but on the contrary a strange mixture of images and concepts emotionalised, which baffles the reader, for here he does not start the poetic journey from the pre-requisite of strictly sensuous means. The action of fusing the contingent world with the ideal world, the action of rising from time to the eternal by giving a temporal form to glim-mers from eternity is the true function of imagination. When imagination operates on the unreal world only, it is fantasy, and when the poet only glides on the surface level of the reality which he describes without living intensely the life of that reality, it is a distortion of reality, a photographic, Parnassian picture. Poetry must be revelation and suggestion of experi-ence, and not description, in however beautiful a style; it must have a character of compulsion and not of obvious artful arrangement. In contrast to the faculty of 'negative capa-bility' described by Keats, the quality which enables the poet to participate in all forms of life, to live the very life of the thing which he contemplates, or the attitude of the 'chameleon poet' of Shelley, Victor Hugo is the 'écho sonore'—a definition which prompted Sainte-Beuve to say: "Qu'est-ce qu'un grand poète? C'est un corridor où le vent passe."[1] There is indeed the difference: Blake becomes the knot in the wood which he examines, and gets so absorbed in this transformation that he ends in frightening himself; Wordsworth becomes the mountain or the cascade which he gazes at, so does Coleridge; Shelley flies with the wind and the whirling leaves, and Keats becomes the sparrow which picks gravel on his window. Victor Hugo is too often the 'echo', mere sound without the substance, the shadow of the real thing drowned in words. Rousseau alone had that faculty of becoming part of the natural phenomenon which engaged his attention. After him, we had to wait for Rimbaud and the symbolists to have that interpenetration of the senses, together with the feeling of the

[1] *Nouveaux Lundis*, tome 8—article on English literature.

universality of life and the absorption of the individual ego
into the 'great One'. Gérard de Nerval was well aware of
what was lacking in our poetry when he said:

> Chaque fleur est une âme à la nature éclose . . .
> A la matière même un verbe est attaché . . .
> Un pur esprit s'accroît sous l'écorce de pierres.

The change in the relationship between man and nature
which permeates English and German poetry and philosophy
of the end of the eighteenth and the beginning of the nineteenth
century had found no expression in French poetry of that age.
I have no doubt that sociologists, historians and philosophers
could account, at least partially, for this time-lag in the growth
of French sensitiveness and French mind; I only wish to state
here that, however slow that growth may have been, it was
nevertheless taking place and showing more and more evident
signs of its strength. Grafting and fertilising by pollenisation
can play an important part in natural growth, but in order
that such operations might take place, the plants need to be
already there, and they need to be alive, so that it is those plants
themselves which have a determining influence in the fruit
which they bear. Spring and growth may vary according to
the latitude of the earth, but a bud which breaks out first is no
more the maker of spring than a poet or a philosopher is the
maker of truth. To be sure, they are signs, and as such they
indicate what is bound to come, and therefore what to do to
meet or to see what is coming; they do give the virtual forces
which ever germinate in the earth or in life their contingent
appearance and a name, but they do not make them. By this I
wish to hint at various conclusions. The first is that a few scores
of years in history, or slight differences in geographical space,
have no more importance than small differences of latitude on
the earth, and yet, of course, those differences constitute our
historical time. The second is that although the growth may
not have come to the surface, it does go on as long as the

principle of life exists in a given place; therefore we must not confuse the obvious bud for the principle of the growth, or for the whole plant which bears that bud. To pass from the general to the particular in history, I should say that one cannot by any stretch of imagination confuse the colours which Poe wore with the fatherhood of the literary movement with which his name is so often associated.

England and Germany had seen these colours and had been wearing them for a long time already, and with striking conspicuousness and brilliance. Even in France, Rousseau had died before Poe was born, and Rousseau had brought to life many of the feelings and beliefs which form the woof and strands of the romantic soul—pantheism, belief in innocence and in the lost Eden and possibilities of union with 'the great One'. Vigny, more concerned, it is true, with his desire to speak about himself, had nevertheless said: "La forme extérieure ne fait que servir de parure à l'idée, consacrer sa durée, et demeurer son plus parfait symbole." In the end, the symbolism of Vigny is not unlike Mr. Eliot's 'objective correlative'; nevertheless it is a form of symbolism and indirectness. Together with Rousseau's name one must also quote those of De Maistre and Ballanche, and that of Sainte-Beuve, who had shown very early his admiration for English romanticism, and his awareness of the distance which separated it from the French poetry of his time. He it was who, before Baudelaire, tried to focus French eyes on the English spring which was already there, and he it was who, although he did not have the force which could have brought to life a similar blossom, could nevertheless feel in himself a similar sap, and detect dimly round him and through him the growing buds. It was Sainte-Beuve who had said in 1830 about poets:

> Ils comprennent les flots, entendent les étoiles,
> Savent les noms des fleurs, et pour eux l'univers
> N'est qu'une seule idée en symboles divers.

155

And a contemporary of Sainte-Beuve, Pierre Leroux, writing in an article published in *La Revue Encyclopédique*, November 1831, shows that symbolism in France was in the air before Poe's doctrines were known:

> La forêt, la montagne, étaient des monuments de la nature; le temple, inspiré par elles, est un monument de l'homme. Et alors s'établit dans le monde une nouvelle harmonie: l'homme ne peut plus voir les colonnades des forêts et les autels des montagnes, sans que l'idée d'un temple à l'Eternel lui revienne en mémoire. C'est ainsi que le monde tout entier, en y comprenant l'Art, qui en fait partie au même titre que les monuments naturels auxquels il s'ajoute, devient *symbolique*.
>
> Le symbole. Nous touchons ici au principe même de l'art. . . . Le principe de l'art est le symbole.

Poets and philosophers, as previously suggested, are both searchers for the true reality; their quest is fraternal and not a matter of influence or derivation. Tennyson, for instance, to a certain extent anticipated the evolutionary theories of Darwin and Spencer. If French poets had not reached the same stage as the English romantics, they were on the way; and in France, contrary to what was happening in England at the same period, the philosophers were idealist and mystical. Knowledge of English poetry in the 1850's and 1860's was, from all evidence, small, but the ideas contained in that poetry were not unknown in France before Poe echoed them and crystallised some of them in a rather elementary and forceful way. "Poetry lifts the veil from the hidden beauty of the world, and makes familiar objects be as if they were not familiar", said Shelley many years before Rimbaud or Poe; as for the belief in correspondences and in an ideal world more beautiful than that of the senses, Keats, in the *Grecian Urn*, and Shelley, in lines such as:

He feeds on the aëreal kisses
Of shapes that haunt thought's wildernesses. . . .
Nor heed nor see what things they be;
But from these create he can
Forms more real than living man,
Nurslings of immortality.

had strongly stressed that belief, echoed by Mallarmé: "La poésie est l'expression par le langage humain, ramenée à son rythme essentiel du sens mystérieux des aspects de l'existence; elle doue ainsi d'authenticité notre séjour et constitue la seule tâche spirituelle."[1]

The dream of innocence, the search for the lost Eden which haunted so persistently the imagination of the symbolist poets and ended with the surrealist experiment in a refusal to accept consciousness and reality, that dream certainly did not appear with Poe but rather with Blake, Rousseau and Shelley, who, in his poem *The Triumph of Life*, shows towards Rousseau the same reverence that Dante showed towards Virgil. Indeed, the whole messianism of Shelley and of the romantic and symbolist age, and the search for the absolute of Rimbaud and Mallarmé came first to light with German idealism and Rousseau, who is, with Descartes and Kant, one of the most important landmarks in the growth of thought of the modern world.

Rousseau is the emergence in literature and thought of that other aspect of the French soul which, for the previous two hundred years, had been overshadowed by the sharp distorting light of Descartes and Voltaire; it is the tumultuous, mystical aspect, the aspect which is dominated by the belief that in the beginning there was only goodness, and that the dream of man should be to recapture, beyond history, the lost Eden. Yet that spontaneous merging of the individual into the mystery, in order to reach the sources, is not as strong in the French psyche as the one which consists in control and consciousness. So that,

[1] Quoted by Ernest Raynaud, *La Mêlée Symboliste*, *Renaissance du livre* (1918–1922), vol. i, p. 59.

in the end, Rousseau is far more attuned to the English genius than to the dominant traits of the French genius, which are above all clarity and consciousness. Indeed, these latter traits are such an important part of the French genius that even the lyricism and the search for mystery of the French poetry of the late nineteenth century still bear traces of acute analyses, psychological researches and conscious control worthy of the classical age; the striking exception is Rimbaud, who thought that even Baudelaire did not go far enough: "Mais inspecter l'invisible et entendre l'inouï étant autre chose que reprendre l'esprit des choses mortes, Baudelaire est le premier voyant, le roi des poètes, un vrai Dieu. Encore a-t-il vécu dans un milieu trop artiste, et la forme si vantée chez lui est mesquine."[1]

Throughout most of French art, the dominant trait is composition and congruence to the chosen main theme, congruence in the name of which the artist ruthlessly discards details, passages of wealth or of extraneous beauty, in order only to retain what is necessary to the whole. The obvious defect of these strict rules of composition and artistic creation is, at times, a certain leanness of the work of art; but then the French language itself is slightly jejune in comparison with the wealth of the English language; and literature is above all language which is the memory of the people who use it, and the most complete embodiment of its genius. There are of course exceptions; there is the exuberance of Berlioz, Delacroix, Rousseau or Chateaubriand, but with these exceptions, how remote we are, until the symbolists, from the natural wholeness and wealth of the Elizabethan age or of English romanticism! Even Victor Hugo's apparent luxuriance is to a large extent willed, it is conscious rhetoric and not spontaneous poetic flowering.

These remarks are meant to suggest that neither the search for the mystery, nor the stress on composition and control, which mark in varying degrees the work of three of the most

---

[1] Rimbaud, letter to Démeney, 15 May 1871.

important French symbolists—Baudelaire, Mallarmé, Valéry—
could be said to have come from outside or could be ascribed
to Poe's influence. These traits are part of the growth of the
French mind, which is itself part of what is called, purely and
simply, Mind. They form a blend of the new apprehension of
reality exteriorised by Swedenborg, Rousseau, Kant and
English romanticism, and of the belief in consciousness and
clarity embodied in the whole of French art. Poe's contribution
seems to me to be very small, very insignificant indeed, unless
we mistake the soldier who carries one of the flags for the army.
"Baudelaire's acquisitive powers were considerable; but they
were not obliged to reach across the Atlantic for material which
lay at hand",[1] says Professor Mansell Jones, who afterwards
suggests that *Le Génie du Christianisme*, "that source-book for
so much in modern French literature", contains strong
affinities with the symbolist theory in a phrase like the
following:

> Le secret est d'une nature si divine, que les premiers
> hommes de l'Asie ne parlaient que par symboles. A quelle
> science revient-on sans cesse? à celle qui laisse toujours
> deviner et qui fixe nos regards sur une perspective infinie[2]

which obviously links up with Mallarmé's essential dogma
that to suggest, and not to describe, is the important thing in
poetry. Chateaubriand had spent many years in England, and
he had been most impressed, as he himself confesses in the
Mémoires d'Outre-Tombe, by the poetry of Wordsworth,
Coleridge, Burns and Byron.

In the essay already referred to, and significantly entitled
'Swedenborg, Baudelaire and their intermediaries', Professor
Mansell Jones' analysis of evidence leaves no doubt as to the
importance of the atmosphere of illuminism and Swedenborgian ideas in which Baudelaire lived; he quotes with

---

[1] Op. cit., p. 20.   [2] Ibid., pp. 22–3.

approval an essay in which Georges Blin remarks that "tous ceux dont Baudelaire s'inspire, tous ceux qu'il a pratiqués ou connus, tous posent ou exposent cette théorie des corre-spondances".[1] What is important for the argument here pursued is the massive evidence of the Swedenborgian belief in the oneness of the universe, in the 'One Man' of Blake or the unity of the cosmos of Victor Hugo, underlying the whole of symbolist poetry; and that belief certainly did not reach France via Edgar Poe, who scoffed at the Swedenborgians; it did not need to, it was already widespread in France in the works of Nerval, of Joseph de Maistre, whom Baudelaire des-cribed as "le plus grand génie de notre temps—un voyant", and above all in those whose author he admired most—Balzac. Balzac was for Baudelaire "a poet and a visionary", Balzac who, writing to Charles Nodier in 1832, advised him to find recruits for the *Revue de Paris* "parmi les platoniciens, les swedenborgistes, les illuminés, les martinistes, les boehmenistes, les voyants, les extatiques, peuple-poète, essentiellement croyant, acharné à comprendre et nullement à dédaigner!" And Balzac's master was Swedenborg. Two of his novels, *Louis Lambert* and *Séraphîta*, are devoted to the teachings of the master; and at the end of *Louis Lambert* he broaches the funda-mental equivalence of sound, colour, perfume and form, and in *Séraphîta* he explains the oneness of man in the angelic state, the oneness of conscious and subconscious, and also the oneness of the universe—a thought which he expressed in these words: "Comme l'a dit Swedenborg, *la terre est un homme!*" Novalis had said: "L'univers est une image symbolique de l'esprit", and: "Notre vie n'est pas un rêve, mais elle doit toujours en devenir un." Shelley had felt before Mallarmé and Valéry that creation, *le hasard*, stains the radiance of the absolute:

> Life, like a dome of many-coloured glass,
> Stains the white radiance of eternity.

[1] *Baudelaire*, N.R.F., p. 107. Quoted op. cit., p. 31.

—Shelley, who believed, without theorising about it, in the interpenetration of the senses:

> a sweet peal
> Of music so delicate, soft and intense
> It was felt like an odour within the sense. . . .

> Our boat is asleep on Serchio's stream;
> Its sails are folded like thoughts in a dream.

That is why we can easily understand what Verlaine, who seemed to have known English poetry better than Baudelaire or Mallarmé, said about Poe: "Quel naïf que ce malin. Je t'en causerai un autre jour car je l'ai tout lu, en English."[1] Verlaine obviously knew that the great discoveries which Poe seemed to have made were part and parcel of the poetry of the English romantics who, faithful to their great English tradition of poetry, placed once more their trust in imagination. It must be said that as early as 1856, in a letter to Toussenel, Baudelaire had realised the importance of imagination:

> Il y a bien longtemps que je dis que le poète est *souverainement* intelligent, qu'il est *l'intelligence* par excellence —et que *l'imagination* est la plus *scientifique* des facultés, parce que seule elle comprend *l'analogie universelle*, ou ce qu'une religion mystique appelle la *correspondance*.[2]

*

What conclusions could one suggest? On one hand we have three important poets of the last hundred years, each one insisting that Poe was the poet who had influenced him most, each one of them having a much higher stature than Poe, and one of them at least—Baudelaire—being more and more recognised as one of the most important poets of the nineteenth

---

[1] Letter of Verlaine to Rimbaud, 16 May 1873.
[2] Baudelaire, *Correspondance générale* (éditions Conard, Paris, 1947), vol. i, p. 367.

century and as the first sign and herald of a period which is one of the high peaks of Western art. On the other hand, despite those impressive encomiums and songs of admiration, we find very few traces of Poe's influence in the poetry of Baudelaire, Mallarmé and Valéry. This is altogether a very baffling situation, something which is not unlike the growth of a myth. A myth is a story or an action embodying some very profound nexus or truth of human life. Each one of the three French poets mentioned saw in Poe an image of himself and of his dreams—none, of course, more than Baudelaire, who discovered his true self in the image of the American poet. And throughout the years, the link between the story and the narrator, between the image and the beholder has become so intricate that we cease at times to see which is which. A perfect instance of how Poe's reputation rests upon Baudelaire and is, to a certain extent, a vicarious glory, is found in Jacques Maritain's book *Creative Intuition in Art and Poetry*, where on page 166 Maritain gives the following quotation, being, as he says, a translation in Baudelaire's own language of Poe's *Poetic Principle*:

> It is the instinct for Beauty which makes us consider the world and its pageants as a glimpse of a *correspondence* with Heaven. . . . It is at once by poetry and *through* poetry, by music and *through* music, that the soul divines what splendours shine behind the tomb; now when an exquisite poem brings tears to the eyes, such tears are not the sign of an excess of joy, they are rather a witness to an irritated melancholy, an exigency of nerves, a nature exiled in the imperfect which would possess, on this very earth, a paradise revealed.

The *Times Literary Supplement* of 25 December 1953, reviewing the book, says that "M. Maritain does well to quote this remarkable passage", and therefore spreads and strengthens Poe's claims to something which he has not written; for the passage is nowhere to be found in *The Poetic Principle*, but can be found in Baudelaire.[1] Baudelaire translated *Eureka, The Philosophy of Composition* and the short stories, but not *The Poetic Principle*, of which he made full use to elaborate an æsthetic of his own. The vital word 'correspondence' is nowhere to be found in Poe.

There are, as we have seen, two forms of influence—the direct and the indirect. The indirect influence, the only one that counts, is not, properly speaking, influence but inevitability. In art as well as in life, it could be summed up in a phrase from Professor Namier's *Avenues of History*, a phrase which says: "The great historian is like the great artist or doctor: after he has done his work others should not be able to practise within its sphere in the terms of the preceding era." After Shakespeare, who would dare to write another *Hamlet* or *Lear*? Keats knew full well what kind of influence that was, when the echoes of Milton's blank verse were such that he had to give up writing *Hyperion*. The poet-dramatists of the end of the nineteenth century knew that kind of influence also, when each of their attempts in blank verse ended in various degrees of failure, mostly because they all summoned the unbearable comparison with the great Master. T. S. Eliot, who has succeeded where others had failed, made it clear that his constant preoccupation has been to avoid using the traditional blank verse and so to avoid conjuring up the great shadow which makes all comparisons disastrous. In France, Voltaire, unable to grasp the meaning of this kind of influence, tried in vain to bring back to life the shadow of Racine without the substance. The point is that once a great achievement has taken place, no further exploration can be done in the same direction. Every work of art is a landmark which can neither be ignored nor repeated: it is there as long as men live, and must always be reckoned with in the course of any further attempts.

1 'Notes Nouvelles sur Edgar Poe.' *Œuvres Complètes* (Calmain-Lévy, Paris, 1896), vol. vi, p. 20.

Considering the direct form of influence, the first point to bear in mind is that art is expression—form, and that literary works of art are therefore closely related to the language which contains them. The Shakespearian theatre means, in that respect, blank verse, just as Dante's *Divina Commedia* means *terza rima*, and blank verse is to English what *terza rima* is to Italian; neither of them is transplantable, least of all into French.[1] As we have seen with the translation of *The Bells*, certain tricks tolerable in one language are impossible in another. Alliterations and assonances are not part of French prosody; jingle rhymes are bad in English and unbearable in French, which is less musical than English. A language implies certain forms of thought and of sensibility, and the prosody of a language is not by and large applicable to another. The orthodox forms which Poe used are as old as literature, those which he abused are not worth being imitated. Imitations of mannerisms and expressions are bound to be, on the whole, confined to one's own language. Imitations from poetry in another language seem to me to be confined to themes, attitudes, responses or means used, but very little to form. As Baudelaire and Mallarmé found out, it was particularly difficult to imitate Poe. Form and content in poetry are one, and a new form implies a new sensibility and vice versa. Therefore the modifications which can be described as purely external are

---

[1] Each language has its tradition and its traits which determine its prosody. French, an unstressed language, is not made for blank verse, nor is it made for *terza rima*, for French is less provided with rhyming sounds than Italian, and one could not strive to maintain, without strain and artificiality, that pattern of rhyme scheme over a long poem. Any individual writer has to operate within the genius of his language, and the best, as T. S. Eliot says, are not those who seek to distort it, but those who extract the maximum power from it. Admittedly certain technical devices can be transposed from one language into another, but that transposition itself has to take into account the whole past of the language and the literature of the language in which the operation takes place. Such a transposition does not reach below the surface. The use of the rhetorical question or of irony, for instance, implies different means in English and in French. Above all, the means of expression, the musical resources, the rhythmic combinations are absolutely inherent to the language which contains them, and cannot be transposed.

few. T. S. Eliot confesses that he was greatly influenced by Baudelaire, yet he says:

A great poet can give a younger poet everything that he has to give him, in a very few lines. It may be that I am indebted to Baudelaire chiefly for half a dozen lines out of the whole of *Fleurs du Mal*; and that his significance for me is summed up in the lines:

Fourmillante cité, cité pleine de rêves,
Où le spectre en plein jour raccroche le passant. . . .

I knew what *that* meant, because I had lived it before I knew that I wanted to turn it into verse on my own account.[1]

He also confesses that he has been influenced by Dante, to whom he paid explicit homage in a book on him, and also by 'imitating' him consciously in a short passage of *Little Gidding*: "For one of the interesting things I learnt in trying to imitate Dante in English, was the extreme difficulty. This section of a poem—not the length of one canto of the *Divine Comedy*—cost me far more time and trouble and vexation than any passage of the same length that I have ever written." [2]

One may quote from a poet and yet know practically nothing but the line which one quotes. Nor is the choice of the same 'objective correlative' a sign of influence. T. S. Eliot has used the symbols of *The Waste Land* and *The Magi*, yet other poets will come who will use these same symbols with different validity. Mallarmé has used in *Igitur* some of the imagery of *The Raven*; but black birds, black wings, black sails have been from time immemorial symbols of bad omen; they are part of an atmosphere of terror and will probably remain so, as long as men remain what they are. One may admire a poet as Baudelaire, Mallarmé and Valéry admired Poe, yet there does not seem to be any poem in the work of these poets

---

[1] 'Talk on Dante', p. 107.   [2] Ibid., p. 109.

which could be said to be an *imitation* of Poe. Memories of readings, images may re-emerge in a poem, as in *Les Fenêtres*, but that is different from influence, something which is, in the end, undefinable.

> There are poets who have been at the back of one's mind, or perhaps, consciously there, when one has had some particular problem to settle, for which something they have written suggests the method. There are those from whom one has consciously borrowed, adapting a line of verse to a different language or period or context. There are those who remain on one's mind as having set the standard for a particular poetic virtue, as Villon for honesty, and Sappho for having fixed a particular emotion in the right and the minimum number of words, once and for all.[1]

Supervielle, in reply to this very question of influence, says: "The masters to whom I owe most? I am so afraid to forget certain names that I prefer not to quote any; and my debt is not confined to writers only. . . . I should be greatly embarrassed if I had to decide whether I owed more to Homer or to the liners which ply the Atlantic between Bordeaux and Montevideo."[2]

Poe stood in Baudelaire's, Mallarmé's and Valéry's minds for certain virtues, a certain attitude to life and art. Poe's influence as a man and a personality is undeniable. Baudelaire saw in him the image of the 'poète maudit', the poet outcast from society—the type which was to realise itself in Verlaine and Rimbaud, the type of which Baudelaire saw himself as a distinguished example. That type had not been invented by Poe; there had been Byron and Chatterton before him. Poe was for Baudelaire the pure poet, the poet who was not "the unacknowledged legislator of mankind"—for that did not

[1] T. S. Eliot, Ibid., p. 108.
[2] Christian Sénéchal, *Jules Supervielle* (Librairie des Lettres, Paris, 1939), p. 230.

matter—but the singer, the nightingale, without any other ulterior motive but his song. Mallarmé's admiration for Poe's personality was more qualified, yet he admired his poetry and his technique just as much as Valéry, who concentrated on the theory more than on anything else. One can see how one can defend or try to emulate a personality which one admires, one can also see how one can admire a theory of writing, but the practice is different both in the theorist and in the one who admires the theory. The facts show that in either case, theory and poetry are two separate things. Of course, every kind of conclusion is possible if one holds such inconsequential views as those of one American critic, Mr. P. Quinn, who recently, in an article significantly entitled 'The Profundities of Poe', stated: "one is tempted to go so far as to say that Baudelaire's life work, his great achievement, was not so much *Les Fleurs du Mal* as it was his Poe Translations".[1] After that there is nothing more to be said; *Kubla Khan* or *The Rime of the Ancient Mariner* would be less important than Coleridge's 'correspondence'.

Mallarmé's conception of music, as we have seen, certainly cannot come from Poe. The interest in horror, decomposition and weird atmosphere had been fully exploited long before Poe by Shelley in *The Sensitive Plant*, by Keats in *Isabella* and *La Belle Dame sans Merci*, and by Coleridge in *The Ancient Mariner*. The preoccupation with death and the fascination of the horrible are part of Novalis' philosophy, who shares with Nerval a keen interest in dreams. The symbolism of Mallarmé is not that of Poe. One can hardly talk of the symbolism of Poe, for it is nothing more than part of the widespread belief in an ideal world where beauty dwells, and with poetry as one of the means to reach that beauty. That form of belief outlined in *The Poetic Principle* is nowhere as vividly felt and beautifully expressed as in Keats' *Ode to a Grecian Urn*. The symbolism of

[1] P. F. Quinn, *The Profundities of Edgar Poe* (Yale French Studies), No. 6, p. 3.

12

Mallarmé is part of his philosophy, his attitude to life and art. On one side Mallarmé is near Shelley, although his beauty is more intellectual and his Eden is neither in the past nor in the future, but out of time; and on the other he is near Blake, with the difference that Blake did not rely on perceptions, but only trusted in imagination, believing as he did in a transcendental world. The existence of Mallarmé's imaginary world is only the distance which separates abolished reality from its projection towards the absolute, it is a duration which is not part of the world, but is only the poet's will embodied in transmuted language, all-powerful and representing all that has been—that is to say, creation. Igitur, "en absolu qu'il est", says: "L'infini sort du hasard que vous avez nié."[1] The poem in Mallarmé is the poet: "moi projeté absolu".[2] The poet, in his act of replacing creation by his will, repeats God's act, is the equal of God. That was Mallarmé's dream, the dream which fuses into oneness absolute subjectivism and the transcendental ego. Nothing is, which is not the absolute subject; and the subject annihilates reality and bases his existence on his attempt to reach, from willed non-being, a mode of being which is the creative act and which, therefore, makes the poet self-created like God.

It seems to me that this artistic belief of Mallarmé has nothing much to do with Poe's æsthetics which is part of the æsthetics of his time. In the same way, Mallarmé's attitude to art is best understood as part of the history of the time when he lived. Then one realises that such an attitude is neither singular nor self-born, but part of a vaster pattern, and not an altogether abnormal development. In Mallarmé's time, artists and philosophers were more acutely aware than ever of the gap between the dream and reality, the machine age and the lost Eden, the inner meaning of life and its expression. The faith in the self, in the individual power to master one's surrounding, had by

[1] Mallarmé, op. cit., p. 434.
[2] Ibid.

then broken down and was being turned into cruel introspections. The bitter laughter of Baudelaire and Laforgue at their
own weaknesses, the despair of Pascal—despair without hope,
for religion had been gloriously murdered by science—was
setting in;[1] so was disgust with reality and society, both products of incomplete reason, yet inane witnesses of a world
without meaning. Poets and philosophers, realising this time
more acutely than it had been done at the end of the eighteenth
century that sensorial reality was in the end nothing but a mode
of feeling, turned their gaze inward, into themselves, in search
of the absolute subjectivity where all subjectivities meet. There
indeed was the truth, there and there only, and not in social
relationships and contacts. Only in solitude could Man discover

[1] Christianity, right up to the end of the Middle Ages, is other-worldly; the
Kingdom of God is not of this world, whose contingency upon essence is not
clearly recognised. The temporal and the eternal are linked through grace,
but the temporal is a shadowy, meaningless world accepted as transitional and
whose secret lies in eternity. The turning point seems to be with Aquinas and
the importance of his 'existential' and rational thought. With him the fusion
of Jewish messianism and Greek mysticism seems to be complete. The incarnation is the revelation of the mystery of eternity in time, and the means to
stress the fact that time and history are ways of translating essence into being.
The important point is that the essence of Essence is being, and being can only
be in time, which reveals and gives consciousness to eternity.
   This existential approach to life pervades the Renaissance and the Reformation and underlies the historical progress which took place from then on to
our time. The importance of history begins with the end of the Middle Ages.
History is human time. Renaissance man is over-concerned with human time
to the neglect of eternity. The Reformation stresses the importance of time
and history—the coming of Christ and His redemptory death are the crucial
events of human life. History becomes the crux of eternity. Contrary to
Hinduism, which is a kind of life-denial philosophy, or to Platonism, which is
a negation of history and of the contingent world, from the Renaissance and
the Reformation onward Christian thought is existential. So is the rising
scientific spirit which moved from speculation to essentially empirical
observation and achieved full consciousness in Descartes, who, together with
his age, retained his belief in transcendence. But the means slowly becomes the
end; history and time, the objects of man's preoccupations, take the place of
eternity; transcendence is forgotten, only immanence remains, embodied in
reason as in the age of enlightenment, and in feelings in the romantic age. By
the middle of the nineteenth century history has become the object of man's
worship, who passed easily from Hegelian anthropomorphic light to the
Nietzschean night of the Death of God. After that we have despair, man-made
transcendence and various forms of flights into unreason.

his true self and the meaning of life; and it was only through that ascetic search of the self, whatever suffering the search might entail, that the artist could contribute to society and to history. Thence the monastic life of Flaubert, thence the excruciating introspections of Baudelaire or the final rebellion of Rimbaud who, when he felt that he could no longer bear the torture of his inward gaze, turned to action to deaden the groans of his soul—the meeting-point of all souls. Thence also the sense of doom and the sense of guilt taken on by the artist who knew himself to be the conscience of the amorphous mass which surrounded him, and who knew that by his suffering, by being the scapegoat, he could atone for the failings of mankind. So the artist became the priest. Reality having proved intractable, reason having failed to bring about the millennium, and the world having been found, contrary to Hegel's views, irrational, truth would have to be subjective. The whole problem of romantic man had consisted in trying to project himself out of the present, but the dream world of the romantic, whether it was Eden or the millennium, was a world viewed from the present and based on reality. The next step was to put an end to disillusions and deceptions and to negate reality altogether, relying entirely on one's own self-created world.[1] The result was, as we have seen, pure subjectivism entirely based on language. That attitude was neither held by Mallarmé alone, nor reached by Mallarmé without precedents. There are, as T. S. Eliot has suggested,[2] lines of development which show the transition from the interest in subject-matter of the earliest poetry to a balance between style and subject-matter and an over-concern with expression to the neglect of subject-matter. That stage was reached towards the end of the nineteenth century, the age of increasing self-consciousness, the age of anxiety, the age of development of

[1] Even that is purely 'a fiction', for if it becomes an absolute belief we have madness, as in Nietzsche, and suicide, as in Nerval.
[2] *From Poe to Valéry*, p. 25.

psychology, psychoanalysis and of the importance of subjectivism and dreams. It was, one must remember, the age of
synæsthesia, of symbolism and of the simultaneity of 'états
d'âme' of Bergson. The only art which at that time could
attempt to convey such an interdependence of feelings and
things was music, the most complete of the arts, music which
was the perfect expression of the Idea of Plato. Therefore
language had to be used musically as the means to discover or
to bring to life the idea. Flaubert believed that there existed
one form only for each idea[1] and that the writer must strive
to find it. Thence his struggle for *le mot juste*. The expression,
the form was all, for it was the unique idea. From such an
attitude towards language to that of Mallarmé, there is not
much difference, there is only one step, and Mallarmé took it.
The step was that if one could discover the *essential* meaning
of the word, one could discover the thing itself, and also that
since there was equivalence between thing or idea and the
word, as with matter and energy, the sum of created things
could be replaced by the word, the long-dreamt-of magic
book of Mallarmé. Before Mallarmé, Rimbaud had propounded the demiurgic power of the poet and the creativeness
of the *logos*. Before them, Nerval had said in *Aurelia*, II, vi:
"Mon rôle me semblait être de rétablir l'harmonie universelle
par art cabalistique et de rechercher une solution en évoquant
les forces occultes des diverses religions." Of course Poe, also,
wrote about the power of words; all poets from Villon to
Shakespeare and Yeats believed in some such power. But
Mallarmé's transcendental beliefs are, as we have seen, very
remote from Poe's search for indefiniteness and ideal beauty.[2]

Just as the heliotrope turns towards the sun, in the same way

[1] Valéry, *Variété V*, 'Mémoires d'un poème', p. 95.
[2] In the end, poets must be granted the right to stand on their own, as
Hopkins, writing to Patmore, said: "I scarcely understand you about reflected
light: every true poet I thought, must be original and originality a condition
of poetic genius; so that each poet is like a species in nature (not an *individuum
genericum* or *specificum*) and can never recur."

genius turns towards the light which it needs, and seeks to absorb the elements which will make possible its growth. Mallarmé was bent on a journey which obviously he would have made and in fact did make without Poe. The knowledge that another traveller had taken a similar road encouraged him and helped him by the trail he left behind. But Mallarmé soon overtook all forerunners and reached bourns which no human being had ever visited before; from these all he could do was to shout to his faithful disciple, Valéry, not to try to reach him who was already on the verge of the unavoidable abyss, but to leave him where he was and to continue his journey alone along a path which was still open. Has Mallarmé's sacrifice been in vain? Far from it; he certainly trod lands untouched by any human foot, and he met his solitary end in a lonely place, yet a place whence, from now on, his great soul shines as an inspiring and also as a minatory light, urging other travellers to go on with courage, but warning them not to push courage to the confines of suicide.

Appendix

CREATION is a whole in which all parts are inextricably bound together. The search for God takes various forms, some being contradictory yet none mutually exclusive. The various religions are all attempts made by men to reach an awareness of God. They vary in spirituality according to the degree of individual or ethnical genius or essence which informs the search. Truth is one at the centre and multiform in its existential manifestations; there are many roads to it. Men worshipped Zeus and Javeh before they worshipped Christ, but they come nearer and nearer to Him, even the professed atheists, if they believe in His central principle of love and human brotherhood. The fact that the apex of spirituality has been reached through Christ—the perfect incarnation of the Divine—does not confer upon any of His followers the right to feel that they are the chosen few and to pronounce a kind of exclusion upon all others who are not in the same position or who do not belong to the same religion. The fate of those who are not so should only call for commiseration and prayers from those who feel that they are nearer Christ, but never for pride—something which destroys the very basis of the Christian faith. The nationality of Christ, the place where He was born and the time when He was born cannot be a source of pride to the people of His time or to the people in whose midst He was born. Social explanation might suggest that the conditions were such that He had to come; this kind of explanation is of the order of: "The light is light because it illumines", and it is merely an attempt to explain causes by their effects and by what is an infinitesimally small number of observable facts when one compares them with the infinite number involved and which are beyond human grasp. The metaphysical explanation, the one which consists in saying that a people has been chosen to be the witness of such a manifestation of the Divinity on earth, is not only irrational but implies motivation and anthropomorphic partialities irreconcilable with the immutable laws and the perfect justice of God. It is a doctrine which fits with the urges and needs of a fighting and oppressed people like the Jews, but which cannot be applied to Divinity without turning the concept of God's majesty and impartial love towards all creation into an unacceptable concept of ethnical paternity and preferential treatment. The Jews happened to occupy a given point in geographical space and in historical time, but they did so as part of a pattern which involves all that preceded. One could indulge in merely rhetorical games and say that if the Pharaohs had been kind to them, they would have stopped in Egypt, and Christ would have been an Egyptian, but the Pharaohs were not kind, they could only be what in fact they were. Plato, Alexander, the Roman Empire, all were necessary to the coming of Christ, and none of these individual or historical manifestations was self-willed.

The coming of Christ to earth, the emergence in creation of God in a form apprehensible to men so that they could unmistakably hear His voice, see Him and follow His message from then on, was determined, in the same way as the emergence of a subterranean river at a given point of the earth is determined by the river's course and by the various layers of soil which it has to go through. That point is a matter of unavoidable laws and not a matter of choice by the soil or the river; they both are what they are, part of a pattern beyond them. The Middle East was, so to speak, the place where the soil was most porous; therefore signs of the divine waters running underground became more and more obvious or visible in that part of the world, which in space ranges from Greece to India and in time from Socrates to Christ; but these signs of moisture and preparations for the emergence of the divine spring were not the makers of the spring, they were merely the climate and the media through which it emerged. The word 'Jew' is only an historical name; the Jews were not God-made as Jews, they were descended from other men, going right back to the origin, to the very fount whence all men came. The idea of a chosen race born to bear Christ could only be made rationally acceptable if the relationship between Christ and Adam through the various patriarchs were direct, based on a short span of time, at least historical time, and exclusive of any other form of human life on earth; we would therefore have to accept the illusion that mankind was approximately 6,000 years old and that it was originally confined to the twelve tribes. In truth, Christ was born with Adam, and Adam is neither a Jew nor a Greek or Hindu, he is man. The historical filiation of Jesus, the attempt to dress Him up in royal rags from the house of David or any other house, seems to me senseless, for these rags are merely part of a very human paraphernalia and of attempts to confuse history with eternity; the King of kings does not need to be descended from earthly crown-bearers, He is descended from God through man, king enough in His misery and suffering, and He is anointed by the faith that His Maker will not, cannot forsake Him. Christ took on manhood, not royal rags. Mary was the instrument of the Lord, therefore transformed, transfigured by the invasion of essence into the purest of human beings, without any need of trappings and vague attempts to give her a husband of royal lineage, something as unnecessary in this case as a propeller to an eagle. She is above all the feminine, the womb which makes creation possible, and the vessel through which divine grace worked.

The transition from God to man, the passage from infinite to finite, from essence to existence contains limitations which make man's complete understanding of God impossible. However God-obsessed man may be—and he is and will always be so, consciously or subconsciously—he cannot through his finite mind fully grasp the idea of God; yet the search goes on, for God, absconded or present in man's conscience, cannot but compel the search. Creation is movement in contrast with essence, whence it originates, which is both movement and non-movement, and it is a progression towards the greater and greater purity of essence. Being in time becomes more and more permeated with essence, which is both the source and the end of being. We may not be aware of the presence of essence, we may, judging from historical and social standards which cannot reach the roots, believe that we have lost the way, that we are bogged in evil, but there cannot be any loss of way or regression; we are merely unaware of the unfailing movement, and the greatest confusion and evil are caused by our pretences of knowing and by our trying to apply data and forms of knowledge, which are only valid at a superficial level of social life based on agreed conventions, to the great stream which unfailingly carries life forward. In that stream the names of the drops or of the banks along which they pass with greater or lesser speed are human names, not God-given names. God gave the source, the initial impetus which contains all and which every now and then, at pre-seen spots or through fore-seen individuals, emerges into human consciousness and time; but He is not, He cannot be actively interested in categories and individuations, which flow from and are informed by the source. These individuations, as they are at the extreme end of the finite, have in virtue of their remoteness from the centre a certain form of spurious independence based purely on the interplay and fleeting relationship of these various termini. For instance, a faint breeze can stir the leaves of a tree, but does not move the branches and even less the stem; yet they are all part of the tree, and both tree and breeze are part of a greater whole informed with the supreme will.

Time or existence, part of essence and apprehended from existence, is movement, growth and change; yet from the point of view of essence, all is simultaneous at the same eternal time and is seen eternally at the same single glance. Creation is not a vast film which its maker has to unfold square inch by square inch through the span of time, it is something which the Maker does in one single act and sees at one glance from the first breath of life to its end. The glance which can view all things at once must not be construed into an infinity of hands guiding each thing to its appointed place along its appointed tracks. Each thing follows its appointed road because of its source; the springs of each action, each movement, each manifestation of life are contained in what preceded, a process which through an infinite regression brings one back to the source, the primal mover of creation. The oak is in the seed, its size depends on the soil where the seed falls—the geographical place, the local winds, etc.; none of these things depends on hazard. For instance, the wind which will blow a given seed to a certain place is itself the result of a concomitance of forces which, if not precisely definable by the human mind, are nevertheless measurable to the finest unit by a mind which could grasp all the data. The trouble is that, as we do not know and can never know all the data, we ever ascribe the missing links to hazard, free-will, or, worse still, to so-called influences which are nothing more than an infinitesimally small selection of data made in order to account for an event which is looked at from a purely human point of view, and which as a result is arbitrarily isolated from an infinite number of causes reaching back to infinity itself. Therefore all our judgments and explanations of causes and, even worse, of motives of actions, are sheer arbitrariness and presumption in as far as they attempt to be dogmatic.

Every aspect of human behaviour, social, historical or even individual, except the purely instinctive reactions at the level of mere physical reflexes, is rooted in causes, in ramifications whose complete analysis is beyond the human mind. The reflexes also have causes, but they can, up to a point, be scientifically analysed, described and related to basic laws whose workings are known but whose true essence is beyond human grasp. The attempt to explain the reactions of an individual or a society according to his or its background and its time can only be made by drawing round them arbitrary lines isolating them from the vast, and in the end infinite (from the human point of view), context to which they belong. This unavoidable process simply means that any examination of individual actions or historical movements is bound to be limited by the power of the imagination applied to it, by the time involved in order to carry out such operations, and owing to the fact that the human mind cannot focus its attention on many things at the same time, it takes place not as if from above (something which would reduce the margin of error) but in a kind of linear way, one thing after another, and generally with more intellect than imagination. The incapacity to embrace wide fields, the tendency to concentrate on causes which are most obvious and closest to us in time, generally ends in overstressing two aspects of life which are merely illusory—hazard, and individual free-will. It is evident that the attempt made by Taine to explain human character and behaviour by race, milieu and time is, unless he had in mind the endless causality involved in these three elements, a most fallacious attempt to impose pseudo-scientific laws upon phenomena which are beyond such laws. All these elements are historical elements whose roots go back to the beginning, and the limitation of the area of examination is arbitrary and all the more dangerous that its conclusions are imprint with a pseudo-scientific dogmatism. The mineral world can, up to a point, be encompassed in laws apprehensible to the human mind, but the animal world, on the whole, defies laws. The only valid method which offers the maximum results with the minimum of errors is that of statistics and probabilities.

I do not by any means suggest a mere camera-like recording of facts; that can be done by the lesser minds, by those who have perseverence to see and to hear what goes on in the phenomenal world and who can faithfully record it. The true historian or the philosopher, for a good historian must be a philosopher, needs not only to be endowed with a powerful intellect able to analyse and to expound knowledge in its discursive form, but also, like Plato, Descartes or Kant, to be capable of those intuitive flights which connect man with the immutable truth of things and which form what we call wisdom. That kind of truth, the 'noumenon' or the 'idea' which informs the phenomenon and gives it its reality, can only be grasped, as Descartes knew, in God's spirit, and is an existential aspect of the supreme, ineluctable will which, by being brought out into human consciousness, produces joy and a quickening of all human faculties and activities towards the fulfilment of essence. The great philosopher possesses not only the intuitive apprehension of truth which characterises the poet, but also the means to expound it logically and through concepts and notions in a way apprehensible to mind. Such explanations, carried out through specifically mental processes, must necessarily shed by the way a good deal of the living force of the truth which cannot pass through mental processes, at least through mental processes which, in order to be apprehensible to other minds, have to deal less with ideas than with concepts and therefore bear the mark of the human minds which shape them. Poetic truth, presented in concrete form with the kind of organic wholeness which symbols and living images axled on creative melody have, retains far more of the true reality; yet although its effect is more pervading, more suffusing throughout time, it is less accessible to mind and as such it is rejected by a greater and greater proportion of humanity tending to equate truth with logic. What is required in order to approach truth is humility and wisdom, and not the pride of 'one-eyed reason' or the wizened sceptical outlook of people who think they know because they can deny the reality of what cannot be moulded into logic, and who think they control events and human life because they have found for them names or have gleefully surrounded them with what they call psychological and sociological explanations whose shallowness is in direct ratio to their self-assurance.

The great wisdom is to know what is unavoidable: "in la sua voluntade e nostra pace". That kind of truth, the only one which is valid, has nothing much to do with rationalising, conceptualising or with explanatory processes which are merely attempts to impose the mark of a human ego on the *per se* of things. Truth may be reached at the point where the individual ego merges into the universal 'I' whose wisdom or direction can be ignored but not deflected. The supreme freedom, the freedom of the saint, of genius, or of the hero as myth-maker, is the freedom of beings dedicated to the spirit or supreme will, which their hearts cannot deny. Christ and the saints cannot deny God; their freedom, the only true freedom, consists in the conscious acceptance of their destiny. Their will is intent on the realisation of their essence, which is the existential individuation of the supreme will—an individuation which retains some identity in eternity. Nevertheless, the belief in the infinite, in the unavoidable will of God does not preclude a certain form of freedom based on human conventions, agreements and acceptance of the fact that as long as we confer upon observational knowledge nothing more than a relative value, that knowledge can be valid and can make possible the exercise of judgment and of a form of free-will inscribed within these accepted recognisable conventions. There is the immutable flow of creation towards its finality which is absolute good, and there are, on the top of it, all kinds of effervescences and ripples—the contingencies of existence, which are so remote from it as to have practically no more influence on it than petals or straw upon the mighty river which carries them forth. Still, petals and straw are what they are and where they are as part of a pattern which they cannot alter. Social life and conventions are bound to be structurally the expression of the essences; they change with historical time and they offer a certain kind of relative freedom, which could be expressed by the analogy of a game of chess whose scope could be expanded or narrowed, according to the size of the chess-board and the number of pieces involved—size and number which, if one wishes, could be imagined as tending towards the infinite and therefore being beyond the human mind.

The problem of a relative human freedom is a problem of individual and social consciousness based on language and on strictly rational conventions. At the phenomenal level accessible to the senses and to reason, there are possibilities of analysable, observable data which are psychological and physical, individual and social. We can observe and measure all the phenomenal aspects of a tree, including the sap which seems to carry life, yet we do not know and cannot know, in spite of the names and the pseudo-explanations which we use, how this sap turns into flowers and leaves, or what is the true difference between a plane tree and an oak; in short, we can describe life, we do not know what it is. Therefore as long as human observations, scientific or otherwise, remain at the level of observations, they are valuable and they make possible certain statistical predictions which increase in certainty the more one comes near to the purely physical world; but they become dangerous if they are turned into explanations involving causes which are beyond our grasp.

In the end, man's fundamental problem consists essentially in trying to know and to accept what is, and thus by so doing to contribute to the harmony of life. The empirical knowledge which is part of life's conventions and of life at the level of observable facts, is only useful if it does not become an end in itself, a source of worshipping concepts such as historicism, scientism or materialism, and accepting them as being full and complete explanations of life. In brief, it is only useful and valid within the limited range of freedom in social life, and it is only so if it is informed with the wisdom that we are part of a whole and that pride, which the Church rightly considers as the major sin, is the surest barrier to wisdom, which can only be attained through the awareness of man's finitude and in the light of the spirit.

The acceptance of the fact that an event or a thing can only be what it is, must not be viewed as a plea for fatalism or for a denial of values, whether social or historical. Neither does it mean that whatever is can only be good. Life is a vast pattern of opposites, of positives and negatives, of blacks and whites, of what is historically described as good and bad. Essence alone is pure goodness, time contains all the aspects of life and is the means of resolving all into the purity of the essence; the process will last until that final purity is reached. One cannot know the relative value of positive and negative, good and evil at work in individuals or society until these forces have coalesced into actions or human behaviour. Nobody except God could know who was Judas until Judas had done his deed, yet he was part of the same necessity as Christ, and he had to do what he did. But he had to do it in order to exteriorise evil, in the same way as Christ exteriorises goodness; he was in fact a part of that transcendent goodness which can only be reached through the absolute awareness of evil which therefore entails at the same time its rejection. I do not mean to say that the awareness of evil on the human plane automatically entails its rejection; far from it. I mean to say that knowledge of evil makes the attempt to avoid it possible, for just as one knows what is good as having been revealed by Christ, in the same way, once an individual truly knows what evil is, he is bound to strive to come nearer to Christ. Therefore, though things are unavoidably the result of their causes, their reality makes some of their causes apprehensible to consciousness, which is a quickening process towards the final good. The more one becomes aware of evil, the closer one draws to the very root of evil—Satan, a metaphysical perversion or a misdirection of the good, necessary to the concept of good—the closer one is to the source and so to the possibility of being integrated into the whole. Satan can only disappear when that part of God's will which is God-made creation has returned to pure essence, non-will and non-being.

One must not confuse the awareness of evil—which on the metaphysical plane is also the nearness to Christ, the gap of despair which stimulates the wings or attracts the inrush of Christ—with all forms of social evils—the greatest of all being killing, whatever the motives involved or the explanations given. It is utterly impossible to reconcile Christianity with any form of killing. One may argue that we have to defend our civilisation, that we must fight or perish, but when we do so we can no more claim to uphold Christianity than could the Church through the Inquisition or any other forms of religious persecution. If we believe that all creation is part of God, we are bound to believe that any kind of killing or torturing or men whom we describe as good or bad is a matter of cosmic significance which interferes with the Divine. Violence in all its forms can only be upheld in the name of philosophies which, whatever their denials, limit man's life to time. The revolutions to bring about the millennium, or the Crusades to restore the lost Eden, as well as the wars to teach people how to worship God and Christ, whether these wars were carried out by Catholics or Protestants, can only take place in the name of creeds which worship time not as a transitional way to eternity but as an end in itself. If in Roman days martyrs died as witnesses of their faith, all those who from Joan of Arc to the Albigenses or other sects were burnt as heretics were also witnesses of their faith, and in as far as they died the victims of a force greater than theirs and which by its action denied the very meaning of Christianity, their death conferred upon them the crown of the oppressed and brought forth the tears which one must ever shed at misguided zeal, or worse still at a manifestation of evil disguised as good. Killing in whatever form it takes place in society is a distortion of God's laws, a distortion which is part of the evil inherent in life and which society always explains in its own way and according to its own needs and designs. Life is a continuous process of making nothingness; fruit, flowers, trees rise and fall; animals feed on one another in a closed circle which returns all things to the whole. Death is a necessary part of life, but killing at the individual or national level cannot be justified in the name of the natural order or made to square with Christian principles. When such an attempt is made, it is obvious that the society which makes it, has taken the path of evil. What should be the reaction of true Christians to it? There is no doubt about the answer, which should be that, although there are vast numbers of good Christians, there is no truly Christian society; therefore such a claim should not be made, for by so doing one tries to bring Christ down to the human level. If a society, like the Communist society, has adopted wars and revolutions as a means to achieve its aims, we should above all endeavour to cope with the roots of such an evil at home and around us, so that the basis of aggressiveness might be eliminated, and so as to persuade that society that it is the spirit which informs matter, and that sheer brute force, whether Spartan, Russian or other, is not the power which shaped history; that there is in fact no pure materialism, dialectical or other. One cannot rule out the possibility of a gesture in self-defence as part of a natural process to protect life (as St. Peter did, for instance), but one must avoid taking upon oneself claims of righteousness which nobody can truly make and which not only bring upon us the sin of pride but prevent us from examining the very causes involved in the aggressiveness of certain societies and individuals. Crusading, whatever the ideal involved, is a thoroughly human and not a Christ-sponsored operation. Whether the aim be Jerusalem or Moscow, no amount of Papal benediction or oratory about democracy and ideals could transform such pursuits into true Christian undertakings. The Marxists, who misguidedly believe in brotherhood by blood, at least make no pretence about their crude beliefs and couple their faith in violence with a denial of God.

Whatever choice we make, in order that such a choice might be free, it would have to be preceded by the complete freedom of all the various circumstances which form its ambient atmosphere, plus a perfectly free choice of the chooser choosing himself, or rather a chooser starting from a state of perfect void and pure will. This obviously leads us back to infinity and God. There cannot be any free choices, since at no time can one conceive of a free-will irrupting into the middle of an infinite pattern and doing exactly what it pleases; if it were so, it would be chaos. All things are inextricably linked in such a pattern, so absolutely beyond any human exploration that the attempt to probe the links between any two actions, however close in every respect, in the end radiates to the infinite. Whatever one decides, one decides out of a field of possibilities which might be partly conscious and mostly unconscious. These possibilities are part of and radiate into the circum-ambient world; what we call the deciding will—a combination of personality and subjectivity beyond consciousness—is itself part of the possibilities which go into the making of the choice, and is rooted in a vast network which, through environment, heredity, physiology, etc., gets lost into the night of time.

In the end, we are driven to two possible conclusions: first, that we can only know the strength of certain forces which form both the personality and the ambient world, once they have emerged, in events and actions. Secondly, that we must accept the fact that whatever is had to be and could only be what it is and the way it is. If it could have been otherwise it would have been so; the irrefutable proof that it could not be otherwise is that it was not otherwise; this is an apparent tautology which has more validity than any form of hypothesis. The 'might-have-beens' are merely intellectual suppositions based on incomplete data and on fancy's flights which are, as far as reality is concerned, meaningless. Anything could have been otherwise from the point of view of an observer merely digressing after the event, but in fact, since the thing was not otherwise, it is quite obvious that it could not be anything but what it was. The differences in possibilities are mental projections of the observer but they were obviously not part of the true possibilities which came to realisation. The past conditional is a tense of repose, a parlour game, a means to satisfy poetic longings and dreams unfulfilled, but it has nothing to do with the reality of things. Nevertheless, since such operations are so much part of the human make-up, one must accept the fact that they too are part of the human necessity—a necessity translated not only in acts but also in smoke left behind as by a train, yet part of the movement which is life. Our thoughts, our images of the world, whether hypothetical or positive or both, are part of our world, they are our means of mental explorations based on language and on the power of imagination, itself the meeting point of end-less unfathomable causes. The wider the imagination to em-brace facts and the ambient atmosphere, the more aware one is of the subtlety of the pattern and of the impossibility of altering anything without upsetting the whole. In fact, the greater the imagination, the more submission there is to the great will which, from the individual plane, can only be felt through non-will and selflessness. It is through the great imaginations of mankind that we know what truly is; and therefore it is to them that we should listen, and above all to the truths of the great revelation of the Incarnation. For it is evident that without the acceptance of the belief that this world is God-centred, that there has been a revelation for all time and that that revelation continues through the various aspects of genius, mankind could try to adopt an attitude of paralysis and fatalism which would not distinguish good from evil and would not be able to differentiate life from death. Just as God—pure essence—came into existence in Christ, in the same way essence, in a less concentrated form, emerge every now and then into human beings, as ignited lava breaks through the crust of the earth. Not all men can be alight and illuminating; few ever see the burning bush, yet those who cannot, should listen to those who can, and not in a mood of sheepishness or bestial obedience but in the light of principles, God-revealed and tested by thousands of years of organised life on this earth.

Selected Bibliography

EDGAR ALLAN POE

The Works of Edgar Allan Poe, edited by John H. Ingram, 3 vols., A. and C. Black, Edinburgh, 1875.

The Letters of E. A. Poe, edited by John Ostrom, 2 vols., Harvard University Press, 1948.

Critical works

Cambriaire, C. P., *The Influence of E. A. Poe*, Stechert, New York, 1927.

Eliot, T. S., *From Poe to Valéry*, Harcourt Brace & Co., New York, 1948.

Huxley, A., *Vulgarity in Literature*, Chatto and Windus, 1930.

Lawrence, D. H., *Studies in Classical American Literature*, Martin Secker, 1924.

Lemonnier, L., *Edgar Poe et la critique française*, 1928.

    Les Traducteurs d'Edgar Poe en France, Presses Universitaires, 1928.

Seylaz, L., *Edgar Poe et les premiers Symbolistes français*, Lausanne, 1923.

Shanks, E., *Edgar Allan Poe*, Macmillan, 1937.

Articles

Arnavon, C., 'Poe, cent ans après', *Les Langues Modernes*, Sept.–Oct., 1949.

Valéry, Paul, 'Au sujet d'Eureka , *Variété I*, N.R.F., Paris, 1945.

S. MALLARMÉ

Mallarmé, *Œuvres Complètes*, 1,653 pp., Edition N.R.F., Paris, 1945.

S. MALLARMÉ

Critical works

Beaussire, *Poésie et Poétique de Mallarmé*, Mermod, Lausanne, 1949.

Chassé, Charles, *Les Clefs de Mallarmé*, Aubier, Paris, 1954.

Davies, G., *Les Tombeaux de Mallarmé*, essai d'exégèse raisonnée, J. Corti, Paris, 1950.

Fowlie, W. *Mallarmé*, the University of Chicago Press, 1953.

Lemonnier, L., 'Edgar Poe et les poètes français', *Nouvelle Revue Critique*, 1932.

Mauron, C., *Mallarmé l'obscur*, Edition Denoël, Paris, 1941.

Mondor, H., *Vie de Mallarmé*, Gallimard, Paris, 1941.

Noulet, E., *L'Œuvre poétique de Stéphane Mallarmé*, Droz, 1940. *Dix Poèmes de Stéphane Mallarmé*, Droz, Genève, 1948.

Richard, J. P. *L'univers poétique de Mallarmé*, St. Seirel, 1961.

Royère, Jean, *Mallarmé*, with a Letter-Preface by Paul Valéry, Albert Massein, Paris, 1931.

Scherer Jacques, *L'Expression littéraire dans l'œuvre de Mallarmé*, Droz, Paris, 1948.

Thibaudet, A., *La Poésie de Mallarmé*, N.R.F.. Paris, 1913.

Articles

Carrouges, Michel, 'Poursuite de l'ombre', *Table Ronde*, Aug., Sept., 1950.

Davies, G., 'Stéphane Mallarmé, fifty years of research', *French Studies*, Vol. I, Jan. 1947, No. 1. 'The Demon of Analogy', *French Studies*, July and Oct., 1955.

Eliot, T. S., 'Note sur Mallarmé', *N.R.F.*, 1926.

Gill, Austin, 'Mallarmé's debt to Chateaubriand', *Modern Language Review*, Oct., 1955.

Lemonnier, Léon, 'Baudelaire et Mallarmé, traducteurs de Poe', *Les Langues Modernes*, Jan., Feb. 1949.

Orr, J., 'Chateaubriand et "L'Après-midi d'un Faune"', *Modern Language Review*, Jan. 1956. 'Mallarmé and English', *M.H.R.A. Bulletin*, Nov. 1954.

Saurat, Denis, 'Mallarmé et la Cabale', *N.R.F.*, Paris, Dec. 1931.

Valéry, Paul, 'Au sujet d'Eureka', *Variété I*, N.R.F., Paris, 1945.

'Situation de Baudelaire', *Variété II*, N.R.F., Paris, 1937.

'Stéphane Mallarmé', *Variété II*, N.R.F., Paris, 1945.

'Le Coup de Dés', *Variété II*, N.R.F., Paris, 1945.

'Dernière visite à Mallarmé', *Variété II*, N.R.F., Paris, 1945.

'Lettre sur Mallarmé', *Variété II*, N.R.F., Paris, 1945.

'Je disais quelquefois à Mallarmé', *Variété III*, N.R.F., Paris, 1943.

BAUDELAIRE

Critical Works

Bandy, W. T., *Baudelaire judged by his contemporaries*, 1845–1867.

Quennel, P., *Baudelaire and the Symbolists*, London, 1929.

Starkie, E., *Baudelaire*, Gollancz, 1933.

Article

Valéry, Paul, 'Situation de Baudelaire', *Variété II*, N.R.F., Paris, 1937.

GENERAL

Béguin, A., L'*Ame romantique et le Rêve*, Marseille, 1937.

Bowra, C. M., *The Heritage of Symbolism*, Macmillan, 1943.

Charpentier, J., L'*Evolution de la poésie lyrique de Joseph Delorme à Paul Claudel*, Les Œuvres représentatives, Paris, 1930.

Claudel, Paul, *Mémoires improvisés*, Gallimard, Paris, 1954.

Collingwood, R. G., *The Principles of Art*, Oxford University Press, 1938.

Darwin, Charles, *Life and Letters*, edited by F. Darwin, 3 vols., J. Murray, 1888.

De Gourmont, R., *Le Problème du Style*, M.F., 1902.

Promenades Littéraires, 5 vols., M.F., 1904–1928.

De la Mare, W., *Early one Morning*, Faber, 1935.

    Private View, Faber, 1953.

Eliot, T. S., *Selected Prose*, Penguin, 1953.

Hunt, H. J., *The Epic in Nineteenth Century France*, Blackwell, 1941.

Hackett, C., *Rimbaud l'enfant*, J. Corti, Paris, 1948.

Lehmann, A. G., *The Symbolist Æsthetic*, Blackwell, 1950.

Lowes, J. L., *The Road to Xanadu*, Constable, 1927.

Professor P. Mansell Jones, *The Background to Modern French Poetry*, Cambridge University Press, 1951.

Maritain, Jacques, *Creative Intuition in Art and Poetry*, Harvill Press, 1954.

Martino, P., *Parnasse et Symbolisme*, Colin, 1925.

Michaud, G., *Message poétique du Symbolisme*, 4 vols., Nizet, Paris, 1947.

Muirhead, J. H., *The Platonic Tradition in Anglo-Saxon Philosophy*, Allen and Unwin, 1931.

O'Connor, W., *Sense and Sensibility in Modern Poetry*, Chicago University Press, 1948. (Pp. 46–7, 68–9, 75, 78–80.)

Peers, Allison, *Alfred de Vigny, Poèmes choisis*, Manchester University Press, 1930.

Peyre, Henry, *Shelley et la France*, Droz, Paris, 1935.

Poulet, Georges, *Etudes sur le temps humain*, Edinburgh University Press, 1949.

Raymond, M., *De Baudelaire au Surréalisme*, Correa, 1933.

Scarfe, Francis, *Paul Valéry*, Heinemann, 1954.

Starkie, Enid, *Arthur Rimbaud*, Hamish Hamilton, 1942.

Symons, A., *The Symbolist Movement in Literature*, Heinemann, 1899.

Taylor, H. O., *The Medieval Mind*, Macmillan, 1925.

    Thought and Expression in the Sixteenth Century, vols. i and ii, Macmillan, 1930.

Whitehead, A. N., *Science and the Modern World*, Cambridge University Press, 1926.

SYMBOLISM

Whitehead, A. N., *Process and Reality*, Gifford Lectures, 1929.
Whitehead, A. N., *Adventures in Idea*, Penguin, 1933.
Villiers de l'Isle-Adam, A., *Axël*, Quantin, 1890.
Wilson, Edmund, *Axël's Castle*, New York, London, 1931.

Articles

Turnell, M., 'Tristan Corbière', *Criterion*, April, 1936.
Berthelot, Ph., 'Symbolisme', *Grande Encyclopédie*, vol. 30, pp. 752–6, Paris, 1902.

INDEX

Index

Index

Montaigne, 129
Month, The, 84n.
Moore, Thomas, 101
Moréas, Jean, 60, 61, 62
Morice, Charles, 60
Mort du Loup, La, 117
Mozart, 13n.
Muirhead, J. H., 20n., 25n., 34
Murry, Middleton, 95
Muse Française, La, 60
' Musique et les Lettres, La ' (lecture), 122–3
My Life and Thought (Schweitzer), 73n.

NAMIER, PROFESSOR, 163
Nerval, Gérard de, 49, 151, 154, 160, 167, 170n., 171
Newton, Isaac, 9, 15, 34
Nietzsche, 49, 82, 129, 134, 169n., 170n.
Ninth Symphony (Beethoven), 132
Nodier, Charles, 160
Noulet, Mme., 70, 71–3, 77, 78, 88, 119, 125, 131
Nouveaux Lundis, 153n.
Nouvelle Revue Critique, La, 67n.
Nouvelle Revue Française, La, 49n., 131n.
Novalis, 160, 167

Ode to a Grecian Urn, 136, 156, 167
Ode to Dejection, 13n.
Œuvres (Descartes), 22n.
Œuvres Complètes (Mallarmé), 51, 68, 74n., 163n.
Origin of Species, The, 30, 32
Ossian, 4
Ostrom, John, 102n.

PALLAS, 80
Paradise Lost, 98
Paradiso, Il, 13
Parnassians, The, 30, 50, 65, 84, 117, 119, 121, 122, 123, 133, 153
Pascal, 21, 22, 32, 129, 140, 169
Pater, 136
Patmore, 171n.
Paul, St., 26
Péllissier, 48n.
Pensées de Joseph Delorme, 151n.
Peter, St., 184
Petrie, Sir Flinders, 33
Philosophy of Composition, The, 72, 85, 97, 105–11, 163

Plato, 17, 19, 20, 24, 27, 28, 35, 36, 41, 42, 43, 44, 45, 54, 56, 102, 104, 105, 106, 127–8, 129, 134, 135, 136–7, 141, 169n., 171, 174, 179
Platonic Tradition in Anglo-Saxon Philosophy, The, 20n., 25n., 33–4
Plotinus, 41, 45
Plume, La, 61n.
Poe, vi–vii, 1–3, 4, 40, 44, 48, 50–1, 54, 63–70, 71, 74, 76, 77, 79–82, 83–91, 121, 124, 125, 127, 129, 134, 155, 156, 157, 159, 160, 161–3, 164, 166–7, 168, 171, 172
Poésie de Mallarmé, La, 70
Poetic Principle, The, 70, 97, 98–105, 162, 163, 167
Pope, 114
Possessed, The, 10
Pound, Ezra, 5, 58
Poussin, 16
Pre-Raphaelites, 33, 99, 114
Prince de l'Esprit, 77
Principles of Art, The, 126n.
Process and Reality, 20, 23n.
Profundities of Edgar Poe, The (Quinn), 167
Propos sur la Poésie, 104n.
Prose pour des Esseintes, La, 68
Proust, 39, 53, 62, 130
Pythagoras, 15, 20, 36, 129, 136

Quand l'ombre menaça, 139n.
Quatre Vents de l'Esprit, Les, 151
Quennel, Peter, 92
Quinn, P. F., 167
Quintilian, 127

RABELAIS, 31
Racine, 8, 15, 16, 21, 22, 23, 104, 121, 150, 163
Rationale of Verse, The, 97, 112–16
Raven, The, vii, 68, 71, 80, 82, 93, 95, 108–11, 112, 134, 165
Raymond, F., 84
Raynaud, Ernest, 157n.
Read, H., 152n.
Read, Sir Herbert, 92
Rebours, A, 57, 60
Rembrandt, 14, 22, 30, 74, 149
Renan, 33
Réponse à un acte d'accusation, 150
Republic, The, 127
Retté, Adolphe, 61n.
Rêve Parisien, 48

196

Index

Vignier, Charles, 60
Vigny, 27, 117, 125, 155
Villequier, A, 151
Villon, 53, 150, 151, 166, 171
Vinci, Leonardo da, 9
Virgil, 157
Vogue Parisienne, La, 89
Voltaire, 8, 23, 106, 149–50, 157, 163

WAGNER, 13, 39, 44, 54, 60, 131–3
Waste Land, The, 59, 134, 165
Whitehead, A. N., 19, 20, 23, 39, 40
Whitman, Mrs. Sarah Helen, 90
Wilde, Oscar, 58
Wilson, Edmund, 1n., 52n.

Wordsworth, v, 4, 7, 12, 26–7, 41, 42, 46,
    107, 113, 114, 115, 153, 159
Works (Schopenhauer), 43–4
Works of Edgar Allan Poe, The, 85n.

XIXe siècle, Le, 60

YEATS, W. B., 2, 52, 58, 59, 103, 116,
    136n., 171

ZEUS, 173
Zola, Emile, 30

198